'This is your mayday book. If you want to start your own resistance, buy *Do Something*.'
Deborah Frances-White, Host of The Guilty Feminist podcast

'An indispensable manual for budding activists by one of the country's most effective campaigners.'
Cathy Newman, Journalist and Presenter

'Kajal Odedra's energetic book is vital for anyone wondering how to map their own campaign. This seasoned change-maker breaks activism down into bite-size pieces with plenty of practical advice. By the time you finish it you'll be wondering why you waited so long to Do Something!'
Sophie Walker, Founding Leader of the Women's Equality Party

'Tired of complaining but don't know what to do? This beautifully written book will not only inspire you but give you a step-by-step guide to creating positive change.'
Magid Magid, Politician and Activist

'Cogs whirring, dominos falling, the digital revolution is changing how we campaign and broadening who can be involved. *Do Something* is a brilliant read, both inspiring and practical.'
Hilary Cottam, Author of *Radical Help: How We Can Remake the Relationships Between Us and Revolutionise the Welfare State*

'I love the book . . . it's absolutely brilliant . . . it's a great read if you feel passionate about something . . . there's so many examples in there of people power.'
Tim Arthur, BBC Radio London

Kajal Odedra is an activist and writer from the Midlands. She has worked in the campaigns and tech sector for over 12 years and is currently the UK Executive Director for Change.org, the world's largest online petition website with 200 million users worldwide. She studied creative writing at Goldsmiths University where she was shortlisted for the Pat Kavanagh Award and her writing has appeared in the *Guardian*, *Independent* and *New Statesman*.

Do Something

Activism for Everyone

Kajal Odedra

HODDER

First published in Great Britain in 2019 by Hodder & Stoughton
An Hachette UK company

This paperback edition published in 2020

2

A CIP catalogue record for this title is available from the British Library

Paperback ISBN 9781529355468
Hardback ISBN 9781529355437
eBook ISBN 9781529355444

Typeset in Bembo by Hewer Text UK Ltd, Edinburgh
Printed and bound in Great Britain by Clays Ltd, Elcograf S.p.A.

Hodder & Stoughton policy is to use papers that are natural, renewable
and recyclable products and made from wood grown in sustainable
forests. The logging and manufacturing processes are expected to
conform to the environmental regulations of the country of origin.

Hodder & Stoughton Ltd
Carmelite House
50 Victoria Embankment
London EC4Y 0DZ

www.hodder.co.uk

For mum and dad,
for showing me how it's done.

Contents

Introduction

'I am no longer accepting the things I cannot change. I am changing the things I cannot accept.'

— Angela Y. Davis

When I was ten my mum took me and my eight-year-old sister to register at our local doctor's surgery. We'd just moved to a predominantly white village in South Derbyshire after my parents bought a newsagent's shop. When we got to the surgery, my mum asked, in her best English, with an Indian accent, if they could register my sister and me. The receptionist made her repeat herself, twice, and then turned to ask me what she was saying. It was humiliating. I remember thinking, *I'm sure the receptionist can understand, why is she making this so hard?* And even if she couldn't, why was she making Mum feel as though she didn't belong?

Back in Leicester where I'd grown up, I was surrounded by people speaking broken English in Caribbean and Indian accents. But in this new village, English was spoken in a thick South Derbyshire accent and you either conformed or were humiliated, as we were that day. My mum was left voiceless, her voice robbed from her by this receptionist. We went home from the surgery to tell Dad that we couldn't get registered because they didn't understand us. We ended up finding another surgery in a nearby village; it was always a little further to travel to get there but worth it knowing we were protecting our dignity.

I was one of two Indians in my year at school, which was very white. We sang hymns at assembly and I pretended to sing along, feeling a bit uncomfortable, unsure why it didn't feel right but knowing I should play along to avoid drawing attention to myself. But slowly I got tired of it; tired of being told how I should act and look in order to be accepted. When I was in secondary school, the uniform was dictated: you were allowed to wear anything that was black, white, navy or grey. When I was in year nine, my parents bought me a lovely baggy grey wool jumper. I loved it; I felt happy in it. Then two weeks later the uniform policy changed and grey was no longer allowed. This seemed silly and arbitrary – if we were allowed to wear grey a few weeks ago, why not now? This new rule didn't make sense to me, and besides, I really liked my jumper, so I didn't mention it at home and carried on wearing it. This caused a lot of distress for the school authorities: tense conversations in the corridor when I was pulled up by teachers for not adhering to the uniform, constant warnings not to wear the thing, stern announcements in assembly that some people had not taken on board the new rules. I insisted. I explained that the jumper was not cheap, that my parents had bought it specifically for school, that we weren't rich, and it was unreasonable to ask me to stop wearing it now in the middle of term – they could at least give us some notice before phasing in a new uniform. If I was in this situation, I thought, there must be others. Some days later I was summoned to a meeting with my head of year, where she accepted defeat and I experienced my first campaign victory.

It was a small win, but I knew from that day at the doctor's surgery that just because an adult held more power, they weren't always right. Challenging my school's rules taught me the power I held in my own voice, a power that I hadn't yet realised. We are faced with choices on a daily basis: choices to speak up, stand up for ourselves, or stand up for those around us. Each opportunity to speak up may not be world-changing in itself, but it is important. This is everyday activism.

*

Most people I speak to wouldn't call themselves 'political', but if I ask them what they think about the area they live in, about their GP, their university fees, about the sexist advert everyone's talking about or whether the minimum wage is enough for someone to live on, I get an animated monologue, impassioned statements of what's right and wrong. We tell ourselves we're not political because we have never really been taught what it means to be political.

Politics is everything. But because most of us never learn about politics at school, our idea of it is what we read in the news and see on the screen. It's politicians and Parliament and prime ministers. It's something very detached from our everyday lives and, quite frankly, unrelatable. And that has a bigger impact – it means we are less likely to fight for what we want. If politics is so far away and detached, it means we can't make a difference.

Some years ago, I ran a series of focus groups with young people across the country to ask them what they thought about politics. What they said won't blow your mind, it's stuff we all know because we've been there, and maybe still are. While many of the young people were interested in discussing issues they cared about or even signing a petition, they didn't want those activities to be seen as political because they felt that wasn't socially acceptable. There was almost an unwritten rule that 'politics' is bad, a common understanding that they all bought into. The way politics is represented in the media reinforces this idea – the polarising effect of party politics, the satire of politicians, the hunger for scandal in the media.

But as we demonise politics, we leave ordinary people feeling out of control and without agency, and end up with power dominated by the usual suspects. Who benefits from the idea that politics is inaccessible? You got it – privileged white men. Look around and you'll find that CEOs, politicians and other decision-makers are some of the most elite, wealthy people in the country. They disproportionately come from the same schools, the same universities and the same social circles. In 2017 from a list of just over 1,000 of the UK's top political, financial, judicial, cultural and security figures drawn up by the *Guardian* it emerged that 97% of Britain's most powerful people were white, even though 13% of the UK population has a minority background. There are more men called John than the total number of women in the FTSE 100 index. Eighty-two per cent of barristers went to Oxford or Cambridge, as did 78% of judges, and 45% of leading journalists. And though a mere 7% of the population go to private schools, they take 44% of the places at Oxford, and 38% at Cambridge.*

* Sutton Trust

At the same time, in the age of the internet that we now exist in, we have more access to, or rather are bombarded with, more information about the state of the world around us. This increased transparency about what's going on creates a choice every time we read or hear something: ignore it or do something. This is overwhelming; how can we do something, everything, anything? And about what? There are so many things! It creates a sense of inertia, we freeze. We do nothing instead.

This is why we have to do something. And luckily for us, it's never been easier. For all its flaws, the internet offers people like us power that we've never had before. Power to organise and mobilise. Power to collect voices that together are stronger than the sum of their parts. The kind of power that can tip the scales in favour of what people want. Imagine what you could do with that power!

Without the internet we would not have had the Black Lives Matter movement, which started after the verdict given to George Zimmerman, a Neighborhood Watch volunteer in Florida, who had shot dead seventeen-year-old African American Trayvon Martin. When Zimmerman was found not guilty of second-degree murder and acquitted of manslaughter, Alicia Garza felt personally wounded. She had a brother the same age and build as Trayvon, who was regularly racially profiled.

This could happen to him. She logged on to Facebook and wrote a long post, 'a love note to black people', she called it. It ended with: 'Black people. I love you. I love us. Our lives matter.' After that the hashtag #BlackLivesMatter went viral. Protests started to spring up across the States; as other black lives was taken, the movement grew. There are now over thirty Black Lives Matter chapters across the United States.

Without the internet the tidal wave of the #MeToo movement, where millions of women spoke out against sexual harassment and sexual assault, would not have emerged. Without the internet we would not have seen the movement of young people mobilising for a climate emergency, creating the largest youth demonstration the world has ever seen, with children as young as ten going on weekly #ClimateStrikes, urging their governments to take drastic action.

Each of these movements led to important change. They may not have achieved their ultimate goal, but they have set cogs whirring, dominoes falling. Dr Khadijah White, a professor at Rutgers University, says that Black Lives Matter has ushered in a new era of black university student movements. And the ease with which bystanders now record graphic videos of police violence and post them onto social media has driven activism all over the world. Multiple men have been arrested across the industries of fashion, TV and film as well as in politics and the Church in light of the #MeToo movement. Children and young people are developing a sense of agency through protest with the climate strikes and their protests have led to climate change being forced onto the political agenda across Europe and the United States.

Each of these movements was started by 'ordinary people' who had had enough, and in a moment of passion they raised their voices and those voices created waves around the world. Because, more often than not, our experiences are not unique. There are people across the country and around the world experiencing the same injustices, waiting to be united so they can fight back.

*

There's a lot of negative stuff about the internet but we can use it to strengthen our connection with each other, rather than letting it drive us further apart. We can unite, we can be part of something bigger. That doesn't mean we have to pick up a placard and wave it around Parliament Square. Choosing not to shop at a clothing chain because you know they pay their workers less than the living wage is activism. Writing to your MP about your library shutting down is activism. Activism can be as local as the food you eat and as big as travelling to Downing Street to deliver a petition.

Right now, our lives are being determined by a small group of people who look and act and think the same. They are the privileged elite who became the decision-makers of the country.

This book is for the rest of us. It's an attempt to balance the scales and disrupt the way things have always been. I've spent the last twelve years working as a campaigner, from grassroots activism to the machines of NGO campaigns. It has always struck me that things I was learning were kept from the public, things that we should all be taught in order to really understand our rights and how to shape the world around us. I worked with young people to help them identify what they were passionate about and how to get those things heard in the powerful corridors of Westminster. I saw that when they had adopted a few tips and tricks, it wasn't as hard as it looks to get your issue on the political agenda. I worked for NGOs who adopted those same tips and tricks. It seemed that if you knew what to do, then anything was possible. But nobody was teaching ordinary people this vital information. I've spent the last six years at Change.org, the world's largest petition platform, doing just that. Every day I see people turning to the platform when all else has failed. They realise that once they spread their message far and wide, you don't need to be a certain type of person, a politician or in powerful circles to create change. You just need to know how to use the tools at your disposal in the most effective way to create maximum disruption. I've seen a single mum fight for and stop her social housing estate being taken over by an American property developer so that they could triple the estate's rent. I've seen a group of young people persuade their local council to declare a climate emergency, and commit to drastic changes to help save the planet. And a mother who fought her mixed-race daughter's school after she was told to remove her braid extensions to fit into the school's uniform policy, forcing them to adapt their policy to include Afro hairstyles. I want to tell you everything I've learned about winning campaigns; the secrets that the people in power don't want you to know because the status quo works in their favour; the tools I've learned and tips from the most powerful campaigners I've come across. I hope it will be both an inspiration and a handbook for real change in your life. Maybe there is something you know you want to change but you don't know how. Or maybe this book will be the turning point for you, to start seeing the world with a knowledge that things don't have to stay the same just because they've always been that way.

Not All Activists Are Tree-Huggers (or, We Can All Be Activists)

'How wonderful it is that nobody needs to wait a single moment before starting to improve the world.'

— Anne Frank

To most people, activism is a word that is over there in the realm of placard-waving protests and police arrests. To quote someone I know who started off thinking he was not a campaigner and went on to force the Home Office to change their mind about a decision to deport his friend, 'I thought campaigners were people who hugged trees.' His name is Luke and he's from Wolverhampton, far from the stereotype of dreadlocked people tied to bulldozers in central London. More about Luke later, but maybe this sentiment is why, in a world where we are surrounded by so much inequality, we're not all speaking up, taking a stand, *doing something*.

Lucy was just fourteen years old when she realised that she was more powerful than she thought. It all started when she learned the truth behind the eggs she ate for breakfast. For many young people, finding out about the treatment of animals on their dinner plate is when they first realise that maybe 'grown-ups' aren't always right. It can be their first step into activism, only we don't call it activism at that age. It's noticeable, like firecrackers going off. The conscience of children up and down the country gets sparked at a certain stage in their life. Questions are asked at home and in the classroom, the innocence of the world around them shattering for the first time. It's a beautiful thing, the idealism that children possess; we should do more to nurture it. I remember when I was a kid in assembly and our head teacher gave a sermon on treating others as you'd like to be treated yourself. My best friend and I sat there absorbed in his every word, our minds racing about all of the ways we were not treating others as we'd like to be treated. In class, later that day, the topic turned to animals and whether it was right to eat meat. I was incensed. *I wouldn't want to be eaten.* We were vegetarians for days after that. It didn't last, but imagine if we had been given the support and encouragement to take our passions even further. Imagine if we had had access to the internet to find groups we could join, petitions we could sign.

This is exactly what Lucy was able to do when she learned about animal welfare. Lucy was the proud owner of five pet hens that she tended to every day, three of which had been rescued from commercial barns or colony cages. She educated me on the brutality of the egg industry where battery farming had become the norm, and hens were packed into rows and columns of identical tiny cages. In 2012 the EU banned the keeping of hens in battery cages but things didn't exactly improve for hens. They were moved into larger 'enriched' cages, which gave hens a tiny bit more than the space of an A4 sheet of paper. These cages have nest boxes, litter, perch space and some scratching materials – and that can house up to ten hens. Then there are colony cages which house sixty to eighty hens in large aircraft-hangar-style buildings full of these cages. They have the same facilities as the enriched cages and the same amount of room per hen. In each cage of eighty hens there are just four nest boxes.

Lucy wanted to do something. She had learned what had happened to her rescued hens and that was enough for her to take the next step. She did some research and found out that Tesco, Morrisons and Asda were the only major supermarkets still selling caged eggs with no commitment to stop. Sainsbury's and Waitrose, the two other major supermarkets, had stopped years before. So she started a campaign – and went for the largest supermarket in the UK first, Tesco.

She started by writing letters, hoping that if she just got her message to the right person, they would quickly realise their mistake and fix the problem. She found the address of Tesco's HQ, explained who she was and what she wanted – for Tesco to stop selling caged eggs. She told them about her hens and what she had learned about the conditions of caged eggs. She also wrote to animal charities, asking what she could do, how could she help in the fight to end caged eggs? Unsurprisingly, she didn't hear a word back from either. So Lucy changed tack and started an online petition. Within days her petition gained hundreds of signatures, then thousands. She mobilised her signers to post on Tesco's social media pages and demand change.

CAMPAIGN UPDATE

I cannot thank you all enough for supporting my petition. It is AMAZING to see that there are so many people out there that agree with me on caged and barn egg farming.

Over 76,000 people supporting a petition sends a clear message to Tesco that their consumers don't want them selling these eggs.

I think it is time that we ask Tesco directly, on their social media, to do the right thing and stop

---

selling caged and barn eggs. If we all posted on their page they would finally have to stand up and pay attention! There is no way they can ignore 76,000 comments all asking the same thing!

What you need to do:

Please take a moment today to write on Tesco's Facebook page and ask them to stop selling caged and barn eggs.

You can leave your own message or if it is easier you can copy and paste the comment below.

Tesco – over 76,000 want you to stop selling caged and barn eggs – please let's end this inhumane practice! #CageFreeTesco Change.org/TescoEggs

And they did it, in their droves. Think about it; if only 1% of Lucy's supporters took action, that would still be 760 people bombarding one social media manager (on a Saturday). It made a dent.

This is when Tesco started to take notice. They put out a statement:

'We are committed to high animal welfare standards and all of our egg producers must be fully compliant with the Red Tractor assurance scheme, as well as meet additional Tesco welfare standards. Eggs from caged hens are clearly labelled as such, so that shoppers can make an informed decision on what they wish to buy.'

This was a start – Tesco were responding to Lucy. Her petition crept up to hundreds of thousands. Her campaign was now being covered in the national media. She was no longer alone; it felt like everyone was now backing Lucy in her fight to end caged eggs.

Then Lucy had a great idea – to go 'old school'. Returning to her first ever tactic of writing a letter to Tesco, she urged her supporters to do the same. Tesco were inundated with literally hundreds of letters from people urging them to meet with Lucy. It wasn't long before Lucy received an invite to Tesco HQ.

I'm sure Tesco expected it to be a fairly easy meeting. They were meeting with a fourteen-year-old animal-lover and her mother: surely a PR dream? To show they care by inviting a young person in to meet with top execs, without having to make any commitments. But we underestimate young people all the time – they are treated as though they know nothing, but they absorb and remember and understand so much more than we think. They see things clearly, without the adult instincts to rationalise and they challenge without the societal norms that hold us back from speaking up. It is hard to stand up to a decision-maker, especially if they are one of the largest retailers in the world. It would be easy to follow their logic and reason, and convince yourself that Tesco are right and you are wrong. But Lucy, in her brilliant youth, was idealistic. She didn't have these things holding her back. She pushed them on the tough issues. They thanked her for caring. She asked them frank questions. They offered her a blog, on their website, to promote animal welfare. She refused. She wanted change, not PR. It was an incredible feat, for this young girl to come eye to eye with Tesco executives. And what happened next was remarkable.

'From the meeting I didn't really get the sense that they were planning to change. That was back in May, and then last Wednesday I got a call, when I was at school, to say they were going to be making an announcement saying they would stop selling caged eggs by 2025,' Lucy told a *Telegraph* reporter. Lucy's campaign was a victory – this fourteen-year-old had come up against the country's largest supermarket and won.

Passion and authenticity

Lucy achieved in a few months something that food campaigners like Jamie Oliver and Hugh Fearnley-Whittingstall could only dream of. She changed the welfare policies of the country's biggest supermarket, a decision they could not have taken lightly – a decision like this would have a huge impact on business and revenue. I don't even think Lucy knew what she was getting into when she started, and that's a good thing. If you care passionately about something and you know it's right, that's all that matters.

Tactics and strategy and knowing how to argue your point is all stuff you can learn and practise. You can't teach passion, but if you have it, your chances of winning are so much greater.

For the people backing Lucy's campaign, her passion was palpable. They knew she was genuine, the signers supported her through every campaign action and some journalists were with her from day one, and having them on her side was pivotal to her success. Most people are smart enough to sense a lack of authenticity. You see it in celebrity campaigns all the time – a Hollywood actress taking up the issue of education doesn't cut through and have impact in the same way as someone like Lucy speaking her mind and refusing to be ignored. She isn't polished and doesn't have a PR machine behind her. But she cares and is speaking from a place of passion.

If you are a human being then you care about things. If you care about things then you probably have opinions on what can make those things better. Activism starts with caring.

Channelling anger

Another way of thinking about passion is anger. What makes you really angry? The things in society that bother you to the point of seeing red are the things that speak to your values. We often think of anger as a bad thing, an emotion that needs to be shut down and cured in some way.

But anger can be useful. It's how revolutions start and dictatorships end.

People make the mistake of linking anger to giving up but it's quite the opposite – it's a signal that we care and means we haven't given up on hope. Think about the opposite of anger – what does that feel like? It's passive and numb. Anger's opposite is apathy; a lack of interest, enthusiasm, or concern. Apathy is dangerous when it comes to politics because it means you've stopped trying to make things better.

But anger is complicated. If you are a woman, a person of colour, working class or from another marginal community, it is a stigmatised emotion, something we're unable to express without apology. We rarely tell these groups that it's OK to be angry. While white men, for example, are able to display anger and move on, others run the risk of getting labelled 'emotional', an 'angry black woman', a 'chav', etc. We aren't properly equipped to embrace anger and use it productively. Psychologist and executive coach Dr Marcia Reynolds says:

The skill is to shift the focus of your anger away from external circumstances to instead focus on what you strongly desire to change within yourself. Once you commit to your transformation journey, you should shift your focus away from what is missing in your life (evoking anger) to what you want to passionately and positively create (inspiring passion). Determine what you want to end and then make the shift from a negative to a positive expression of what you deeply desire to create.

We can use anger as a tool to help us read situations and research has shown it can actually help us to make more optimistic choices. In 2001, Jennifer S. Lerner and Dacher Keltner published a study measuring individuals' general moods, and then asked the participants to make a series of decisions about how they would proceed in situations where there were high probabilities that many people would be killed – but also the possibility that those people could be saved, too. They found that people who were angry made the more optimistic decisions, aiming to take more risks if it meant saving more people.

All of this isn't to say we should all work on making ourselves really angry every day, but it's important to understand that the emotion has a purpose and that embracing it can lead to great things.

Persistence

If you are passionate or angry, you are more likely to persist with the cause. In my years of campaigning and observing activists, it is those that remain determined, that maintain the dogged belief they are right and that victory is achievable, that are the ones who go on to win. It's about being stubborn and being consistent. This is often the case for those who don't have any other option but to fight. Like Yvonne McHugh.

Yvonne and Billy first met on the island of Barra on New Year's Eve in 2011. He was playing the pipes in a pub. Yvonne went into the pub with a friend and said as soon as she set eyes on him, she was smitten.

'I thought, *Who's the guy playing pipes?* I turned to my friend Paul and said, "I'm gonna marry him, he's amazing." Later on in the night I tried to talk to him outside, but he was so drunk, it didn't go anywhere. I went back to Glasgow and thought I might not ever see him again. But then two weeks later I was at a gig in town and he was there! He came up to me and said, "You're the most beautiful girl in there." I asked, "Are you Billy Irving?" That was it, we moved in together a month later.'

In 2012, just a year after they'd got together, Billy and five other British men, former soldiers, were employed on a merchant ship as security. When cargo is transported across seas, pirates are a genuine danger and so companies hire security firms to protect their boats. When Billy's ship entered Indian territory, they were accosted by the local authorities and before they knew it, the six men were sitting in a dark cell in the Indian city of Chennai, their passports confiscated and no understanding of what was going on. And so began Yvonne's four-year battle for Billy's freedom. They had been arrested for reasons that were unclear. There was mention of not having the paperwork to have weapons on board, but it was unclear as their employer, US private maritime company AdvanFort, claimed this wasn't true. Yvonne was sure these men were being scapegoated, and nobody was stepping forward to help. She contacted the Foreign Office, who she says were great. They would listen to her cry down the phone and call every day with updates on what they were doing to assist. 'They couldn't have been any better,' Yvonne recalls. But that slowly fell apart when the six were first charged, after six months of being held. Then the government stopped returning calls, took longer to reply to emails. 'All of that support we had just fell away, they left us.' The Foreign Office had advised the families not to visit the men in India because it was dangerous; they advised them not to speak to the media because it could put the lives of the men in danger. But when they stopped giving support themselves, out of desperation Yvonne started a public campaign calling on the UK government to help the six British former soldiers.

All the men had families at home in Scotland who had to spend every Christmas and New Year without their fathers, sons, brothers, husbands. Advanfort offered little help, no legal protection and soon stopped paying the men's wages – some of whom had children and wives to support. The UK government was their only hope. Yvonne was pleading with the Foreign Office to intervene and help bring them back home. She was hurt, because they had stopped responding after giving her so much emotional and practical help at the beginning. These boys were ex-soldiers who had fought in Iraq and Afghanistan, devoted their lives to the country, and now they needed our help, but the government did nothing.

Billy spoke of the conditions they were in as he wrote home:

I've been hallucinating while sleeping . . . I'm not surprised anymore when guards are beating people with bamboo sticks or if someone is taken to hospital with a slit throat.

Yvonne went public with as much information as she could. Soon, she had over 400,000 supporters who had signed her online petition, who gave her hope when all hope seemed lost. As the years passed by, people continued to sign her petition, write to MPs, and spread the word across social media. The men were let out on bail but unable to leave the country, making them prisoners of state. But it meant that at least Yvonne could visit Billy for all-too-brief stints. A year of this agony passed and Yvonne got pregnant. The pair were elated and heartbroken, knowing that the chances of her going through this pregnancy alone were quite high. Supporters continued to hold them together; they sent parcels and Christmas cards to the men. The campaign made front-page news and soon senior politicians wanted to meet with Yvonne and the other families. Four years later, finally, the prime minister, Theresa May, spoke out about their plight and soon, after many appeals, they were set free and the charges dropped.

The best time to be a campaigner

I've spent more than a decade campaigning on issues from sex education to homelessness. In that time, it's been quite incredible to watch how the internet has shaken up activism. Quite simply, Yvonne would not have won her campaign without it. When I started campaigning all those years ago, every step took longer. In 2007 at the UK Youth Parliament, we ran the biggest survey of young people about their sex education – over 21,000. That was a big number back then because of the labour it took to gather that data. It required a survey, available online, which had to be printed out in order to respond, and sent back to the UK Youth Parliament headquarters. It was time-intensive to say the least. The whole process took months. The survey got national headlines as young people revealed just how poor their sex relationships education was. The front page of *The Times* read: 'Backlash over sex education failings' and soon after, a government review was launched. Now, with the internet at your fingertips, you could get a survey of over 20,000 respondents in a couple of days. You would just put the questions online, share the link, and let an online tool analyse the results for you. Imagine what we could have done with the campaign in the time we would have saved!

And it's not just surveys. Almost every tool in a campaigner's belt has been ramped up by the power of the internet, particularly with the power of Twitter, Instagram, Facebook and Snapchat. By the time you read this I'm certain there will be another app launched that, yes, we will waste hours of our life scrolling through like zombies but that we will also use to share campaigns with our friends to help build movements. Movements like #MeToo, Black Lives Matter and the Arab Spring wouldn't have had the impact, if they'd even existed, without social media.

The internet has levelled out the playing field for ordinary people and made it easier and far more effective to have your voice heard. People talk about 'clicktivism' as though it's a bad thing, as though the internet is lowering the bar and making us lazy, thinking that we're activists when all we're doing is 'liking' a post. But that's rubbish. Petitions are as old as democracy; for hundreds of years we have been publicly adding our names in support of others seeking change. What's different now is it's just dramatically easier than ever before to start petitions because you can do it online, and spread them through social media.

The term 'clicktivism' was coined to put people off campaigning – because clicktivism is working.

Those in power, whether they are corporations or politicians, have had a huge wake-up call over the last decade.

Seemingly out of nowhere the public has found a way to speak up in a way that is loud, fast and incredibly effective.

Twenty years ago it was harder for the ordinary person to oppose the actions of the powerful, so things stayed the same and progress was slow. If you faced an injustice you either had to put up with it, moan to your friends or commit a lot of your time and money to changing it. Fast-forward to the digital revolution and the way we campaign has evolved. As a citizen, it's our right to challenge the powerful – and now we have been given a megaphone to do it effectively. That is something to be embraced. The internet has opened up a world of campaigning to people who never thought of themselves as campaigners. It's not just about getting a number of people to sign a petition. It's about growing an audience of people who care about the same issue as you, creating a community and growing your power by literally growing the number of people on your side. That is pretty terrifying to people who want to keep things as they are.

And once you get started, you'll realise that the internet is just one string of many in your bow; that the campaigns of today follow the same principles and strategies of decades-old activism. It's just that now your chances of success are much higher – now is your time to do something.

Being a thoughtful campaigner

So, some injustice has occurred, and it either affects you directly or not, but you want to make things right. And if you want to do it effectively, you need to make sure you've thought about the issue deeply. That starts with making sure your activism is intersectional.

Gah, another bit of jargon! I know, I know. When the term "intersectional" started to get thrown around in activism circles, I was totally intimidated. I wasn't sure I understood what it meant, and it felt as though if I admitted that, I would come across as closed-minded, and that my activism would end up being judged. If someone had explained it to me in plain English, I would have realised it's a no-brainer. So that's what I'm here to do. The Merriam-Webster dictionary defines it as:

> **Intersectionality:** *The cumulative way in which the effects of multiple forms of discrimination (such as racism, sexism, and classism) combine, overlap, or intersect especially in the experiences of marginalized individuals or groups.*

In plainer English, it's about the intersection where issues affect multiple marginal groups, not just one. And we can use this to help us more deeply understand the reality of injustice that is often hidden in mainstream media and politics. So if you're campaigning about climate change, you need to consider how climate change affects not just the UK climate and population, but the impact that climate change has on women, people of colour, people with disabilities.

Mosharraf Hossain, of the disability rights movement in Bangladesh, one of the world's poorest countries, and one of those most affected by climate change, says, 'There are an estimated fifteen million disabled people here . . . around ten or eleven per cent of the total population. There is a strong link between disability and poverty. The health service here is poor. Only one in ten disabled people has access to school.' Extreme rising sea levels caused by global warming, flooding, cyclones, subsequent water and food shortages, the risk of being made homeless by violent weather conditions, these are very real situations for disabled people across the world when they are part of the poorest communities.

Did you know that climate change affects women more than men? According to official UN figures, 80% of people displaced by climate change are women and following climate disasters, it is generally harder for poor women to recover their economic positions than poor men.

And as climate change degrades the planet at an ever greater speed, it is people of colour, those in the global south, who will be most impacted. Though the UK is one of the biggest carbon emitters per capita, it is countries like Bangladesh that are the most vulnerable when it comes to natural disasters. These countries typically have less money, because they bear the brunt of global inequality, and are disproportionately communities of colour.

So if a single issue like climate change, which is often reported and debated without nuance, can be this complex when it comes to the impact it has on marginal communities, you can see how the whole world we live in is interwoven in a similar way.

This section feels quite personal for me; as a woman of colour with a working-class background, I've felt that strange mix of relief and resentment when a 'diversity' scheme at work focuses entirely on gender. Or the painful impact of the constant media and public narrative of racism that focuses on the office and boardroom, completely missing the way racism plays out in working-class worlds. Intersectionality is important to our activism because it helps determine our messaging, tactics, and target audience. It's about the world we're striving for. I haven't met a single campaigner who isn't idealistic and hopeful about the kind of future they could help create. So it would be a disservice to your work if you aren't asking yourself some basic questions to make sure your activism is thoughtful and inclusive:

1. How does the issue impact people due to their sexual orientation and identity, gender and gender identity, race, economic status, immigration status, national origin? If you don't know, that's OK – look it up. As a campaigner I spend half my life researching and educating myself so that my work is as empowering as it can be.

2. How do the forms of discrimination intersect with each other and present unique challenges for affected individuals and communities? For example, it is true that air pollution disproportionately impacts people from working-class communities more. It also impacts people of colour more. At the intersection, as a working-class family of colour, how does air pollution impact unfairly? This family is less likely to get access to the health treatment they need as a result of the pollution, are less able to afford to live in a low-emission zone, are less likely to be heard when they need help from services. The analysis of how discrimination plays out in an issue helps us challenge assumptions about our campaigns so that we are not further marginalising people from the work we do, and creating deeper fractures in society.

3. How can you bring in the voices of those most affected by the issue? Intersectionality is not just

about recognising the problem, but also about giving space to those who need it and are often excluded from mainstream conversations. It's about realising the power of those communities, and the work they have already done, rather than trying to be a do-gooder. It's realising that a person with direct experience makes them a leader in the field, a leader that needs to be heard.

The endurance test

Billy and Yvonne recently sent me a Christmas card, a beautiful picture of the couple with their two sons, William, named after his dad, and Hector. I see Yvonne's beaming smile in that picture and remember how tired and preoccupied she looked during those years of campaigning. She was exhausted but had no option but to keep going, with her Glaswegian accent and bright eyes that clung to hope when it seemed in short supply. For Yvonne, she had no choice but to keep going. There were times when people advised her to keep quiet, telling her not to be so noisy, that it wouldn't help their case, and could set them back. But her consistency in keeping the story in the media and online meant that no one ever forgot about the men, nicknamed the Chennai Six. Every

Christmas, Yvonne led a campaign stunt, getting protest messages written on Christmas cards. Every birthday or campaign milestone, Yvonne was there with press releases and tactics lined up. She didn't give up because she had no other choice. The father of her child was in prison on false charges; if Yvonne didn't fight for him, who would?

When I asked Yvonne how she kept going in that time, she said, 'It was hell. But I knew we were supposed to be together. The way we met was so incredible and unlikely, so I couldn't give up after that. We were meant to be.'

At first she could deal with him being away. When they first met he'd just left the army and started doing maritime security work. She was used to him being away for short periods, weeks at a time. But then as the weeks turned into months, not knowing when, or if, the fight would end was agonising. 'Normally when something bad happens you know it won't last forever. I was only twenty-two when it happened, I'd only known him for a year and it was a big gamble to take this on.'

There were times when she wasn't sleeping or eating for months on end.

'I'd sit on the internet day and night looking up articles, lawyers, politicians. Trying to find a way out. It wasn't until I went to see Billy in January, four months after he'd been arrested, that I could settle. I was finally able to sleep since October. Seeing him in person, hearing him tell me to my face that he was OK, that kept me focused and I knew I had to stay healthy for Billy.'

This level of commitment is inspiring. It's also understandable. We are more invested in something if we have skin in the game. This is one of the reasons why people campaigning on issues that affect them and their communities are more likely to be successful (there are other reasons that we'll get to later). When it came to the caged egg industry, Lucy's passion was personal. She could imagine the awful conditions her rescued hens had come from, she felt she *had* to do something. And she hasn't stopped, because the problem hasn't stopped. Once she had dealt with the major supermarkets, she went for the government. Her current campaign is to get legislation to completely ban caged hens' eggs. It's challenging to keep up this kind of energy and motivation for campaigning about an issue when you have no idea how long it will take. It's harder still when you experience setbacks; how can you keep up the desire to continue? You do it by keeping the heart of the issue close to you – keeping the reason you're campaigning at the front of your mind. There will be times when you're doing boring things, like entering data or stuffing envelopes. Or when you're doing something that is draining and depressing, when you have a meeting that doesn't go the way you expected. When you hear doubt and that doubt plants a seed in you, it is likely to grow if you don't remember why you're doing this. Here are some things I've seen help:

Build a community around you

Meeting people who care about the same thing is so important. To exchange ideas, to vent, to lean on when you're feeling defeated. Have people around you that you can call when you need a boost of camaraderie. I think it's the most powerful reason to go to demonstrations; the chances of the decision-maker changing their mind because of a protest are slim but you do it because of the sense of community that exists in that space. They can be incredibly loving events, and there's nothing like building connection out of a fight for justice.

Keep learning and being inspired

Reading books and articles, listening to podcasts, watching films, going to see art that is connected to the issue you're campaigning on will engage a different part of your brain. You don't always have to be writing emails and posting on social media; absorbing things around you is equally important in keeping your brain engaged and your heart in the game.

Collect symbols

There was a time when, after the third court appeal got turned down, I asked Yvonne how she did it, how she kept going all those years. Yvonne faced so many setbacks and roadblocks. But every time I spoke to her, she was a vision of positivity. 'When I first went to see him in India, he made me a ring and a bracelet from the rope of the cloth he was sleeping on. It was a green cotton thing. I wore that all the time. It helped me focus on why I was there. You can lose focus at times, with anger toward the Foreign Office or the Indian government. There were people in our campaign who I didn't particularly like. That ring and bracelet kept my focus – as a reminder that sometimes you have to do these things for people you love.'

She needed to be reminded of the days when they were together, in the same place, how special that was and that it was something worth fighting for. It's so easy to forget why you're fighting when you hear for the millionth time why something can't change, and in those moments you need help to remember. Find pictures, jewellery, make a noticeboard with quotes and phrases, something specific like a stone from a particular place, and keep the reason you're campaigning close to you.

Be you!

Going into campaigning, one of the most tempting things to do is to impersonate the politicians and very serious speakers you see in the media. This is partly because we all have an element of feeling like an imposter, that we don't belong doing what we're doing and that we'll be caught out at any moment. Naturally we think the way around this is to fit in and be like those we have seen before us. Don't!

It's our *experiences* that make us powerful – they're our superpower.

We just don't know it because society projects a very limited idea of what strength is. We're told that power is to be a wealthy white man. But what if we disrupt that idea and step into our perceived weakness?

Here's a final story before you dive in.

Mary is Belinda's mum. She uses a wheelchair due to a forty-five-degree curve in her spine, severe facet joint deterioration in her back, and other conditions. She was visiting her daughter, who was just finishing her first year at university in London. But what was supposed to be an enjoyable weekend turned into a humiliating ordeal for the both of them.

The apps they were using to find their way around the city kept sending them on routes that were not wheelchair-friendly, leading to time-consuming, degrading and sometimes frightening consequences. Can you imagine – trekking around a huge city like London, travelling forty minutes to then be faced with a footbridge and having to go back the way you came and find another route? They wasted hours like this. While Google Maps highlighted accessible Tube stations, Belinda and her mum found that once they exited the stations, it took them three times as long, because the route that Google suggested wasn't passable.

When they got home, Belinda was furious, she felt choked. But instead of accepting she had no choice, she did something. She started a petition – for Google Maps to make their app accessible for everyone, with wheelchair-friendly routes. Just months after starting that petition, Belinda heard from Google – they invited her in for a meeting. Belinda could have been intimidated, but she felt powerful. Her petition had been signed by 300,014 people, and she walked into that meeting with those 300,014 people behind her. Maybe they were going to flatter her and hope she would go away. But Belinda persisted. And Google finally agreed, rolling out accessible Google Maps in every major city.

Belinda's power here was being 100% herself. Her

determined, idealistic, angry self. When she spoke to the media, she never changed her language or dressed any differently. Because what was exciting about Belinda was exactly what we sometimes are tempted to eradicate in ourselves: she was a young person at uni, hurt by what her mum has to keep going through, an inexperienced campaigner with loads of passion.

I have walked into countless rooms with decision-makers, sat at tables where I am the only female, person of colour and person under forty in the room. And I have realised now after years of battling with imposter syndrome and wondering whether I should speak and act like those middle-class, middle-aged greying men, that when I speak up, the more I am myself, the more they are impressed and intimidated. Because I'm different and they don't know what to do with 'different'. Hold on to this:

your experiences will make you the most powerful person in any room.

Making the Cake (or, The Strategy Bit)

'I think baking is very rewarding, and if you follow a good recipe, you will get success.'

— Mary Berry

Before I begin I need to apologise for the heavy-handed metaphor you're about to endure. But I've been baking lately, so forgive me. Ready? We're going to get a bit technical.

Campaign strategy is the theory for how you will win your campaign and you'd be lost without it. There are a million different tactics you could use in every campaign, but they're not all relevant and rather than getting you closer to winning, best case, they will waste your time; worst case, it sets you back further from your goal. So in order to decide what to do, you need a strategy.

And yes, I agree. The word 'strategy' is boring, and let's be honest, it sounds like a lot of work when you probably already have a lot of work on your plate (see the baking metaphor beginning to creep in?). But if you give it a go and have the right approach, I think it can be one of the more fun parts of campaign planning.

Think of your strategy like making a cake (ta da!) – you wouldn't expect it to just happen, to just appear in front of you in the kitchen, would you? You would write lists, buy ingredients, have a recipe that you follow. Campaigns fail when they haven't been thought through and when the same old tactics have been used regardless of who the decision-maker is. You wouldn't put baking soda in every cake you want to make; each cake has a different set of ingredients in order to produce different results. For example, often campaigns focus far too much time on trying to get the maximum number of people signing a petition rather than really thinking about what will persuade the decision-maker. There's a different technique for baking a bread-and-butter pudding than for baking a Victoria sponge – just as there is a different way of messaging your campaign to a politician or to the public. OK, I think I've stretched that cake metaphor to its limit.

Developing your campaign strategy involves answering a set of questions that enable you to think about the big picture. It's not the actual plan, your to-do list or a list of your tactics, but the framework for how you'll win. You make your campaign decisions based on this framework – does taking step X or Y fit with my strategy to win?

It's about putting yourself in the gatekeeper's or decision-maker's shoes, identifying what they value and how you can use what they value to motivate them to agree to your 'ask'. It's about being cunning and mischievous. If you're a person who likes to scheme, you'll be in your element.

The basic questions you should answer to create your strategy are:

- <u>Define victory</u>
  What does it look like to win? Would you be willing to accept a middle ground, what does that look like?
- <u>Understand your decision-maker</u>
  What makes them tick? What would it take to persuade them to agree with you and take the necessary action you want?
- <u>Decide your theory of change</u>
  Work backwards and think about the key steps from victory to where you are now (more on this below).
- <u>Develop and articulate your campaign message to convince them</u>
  What messages will be most persuasive to the decision-maker?
- <u>Identify key supporters you need on your side</u>
  Who else cares about this? Is there anyone that has influence or could help you with the campaign?

Consider MPs, other campaign groups, community leaders, experts and other influential people on the issues, or demographics of the public you need to support you.

What's your theory (of change)?

Halfway through my campaigning years I learned about this thing – theory of change – and it made so much sense I couldn't believe it wasn't being used in every part of life. Your theory of change is *how* you expect your campaign to win. It's how you'll get from 'A' to 'B', where A is the world we live in now, and B is the world where the decision-maker has agreed to your demand. Now start from B, the world you want to see. And work backwards to understand the exact route you need to take, considering the unique position you're in and the resources you have.

Here are some campaigns and their theories of change, so that you can see how different they can be. It may also give you some ideas for what the theory might be for yours.

Legal challenge

When the Bank of England said they would be redesigning their banknotes with the result that all of the historical figures on the banknotes would be men (barring the Queen), there was a huge backlash. The campaign for women on banknotes mobilised public feeling, with a petition and lots of media attention. But Caroline Criado-Perez, the brains behind the campaign, saw a chink in the Bank's actions, in that they had breached their public sector equality duty. Caroline decided to pursue a legal challenge and pin them on this. She started to crowdfund for the case and quickly raised thousands. Before they managed to get to court, the Bank requested a meeting with Caroline . . . and the rest, along with Jane Austen on our ten-pound notes, is history. This theory of change was very smart: the Bank would have looked very silly if they had gone to court over this and they knew it; public sentiment was in favour of Caroline's campaign and it seemed childish to keep fighting when they were asking for something very reasonable.

Divestment

The campaign for fossil-free divestment has a clear theory of change to tackle climate change. Their theory is that if companies reject donations and sponsorships from fossil fuel companies, that will weaken the industry and stop fossil fuel companies from thriving. Every time an institution publicly breaks its ties with fossil fuel companies, the campaign chips away at the pillars of support that allow the industry to carry on.

This theory of change is powerful because it has created a sophisticated domino effect. Every person or institution knows exactly how they can have an impact and as each one pulls out, the momentum builds. It's also incredibly smart to use business as a campaigning target.

Public pressure

Campaigns which have been successful in getting the Home Office to U-turn on unfair deportation orders have relied on mass mobilisation to create public and media pressure on the government. This spotlight on the Home Office often creates embarrassment when the reason given to the individual doesn't make sense, which sometimes means the case is escalated and dealt with immediately. While these cases are often legally challenged at the same time, it's been clear time and time again that public support has influenced decisions to change deportation orders.

Boycott

Professor Samira Ahmed found a unique way to end the second Sudanese Civil War: she called for wives to abandon sexual relations with their husbands. The earliest record of this idea is actually attributed to the Greek playwright Aristophanes and his play *Lysistrata*, where this tactic is used to end the Peloponnesian War of 431–404 BC. The war ended three years after the tactic was introduced. It may not have been completely due to this boycott, but it was a powerful campaign that only the wives could have led.

You can see from this list that you couldn't apply these theories to just any campaign; it needs to be mapped out for each specific issue. And if you don't think about this early on, it can be very difficult to get it right halfway through, because your theory of change impacts everything, from the language you use to the tactics you choose.

The reason your theory of change matters is that every campaign is different. Not all tactics work for every campaign. Not all messaging works for every campaign. Each has a unique decision-maker, unique context, unique opportunities. Your theory of change will guide the answers to the questions in your strategy. It will help you to see the campaign and the big picture clearly, and stop you from going into autopilot and dishing out tactics for the sake of it, ensuring you spend your time and resources in the most efficient way. It is also often the difference between a good and a bad campaign. Do you see what I mean about using it in every part of life? Surely we should be this clever with all of our goals? (For example, I would like to be friends with Oprah; I need to 'theory of change' this immediately.)

People don't often think about this and dive straight into the campaign messaging and getting in front of the decision-maker. But by doing that, you will waste a lot of your efforts without thinking strategically about what your values are and how you can best win.

The campaign to Repeal the Eighth

The campaign to legalise abortion in Ireland was finally won in 2018. In 1983 the Eighth Amendment was added to the Irish constitution, which gave equal status to the life of the mother and the life of the unborn, and since then a campaign was created to have that amendment repealed and give women in Ireland the right to abortions.

In May of 2018, the country voted in a referendum by a landslide, 66.4% to 33.6%, to remove the amendment. I spoke to Ailbhe Smyth, an Irish academic and activist, who was a leading figure in the campaign to Repeal the Eighth, about the anatomy of the campaign.

Since 1983 Ailbhe has fought against the Eighth Amendment. She is a fierce, poised and articulate woman, with cropped red hair that gives her an edge of punk. Her incredible career adds to her radical credentials; Ailbhe has spent decades fighting the Irish establishment since the 1970s, campaigning for the women's liberation movement and gay rights. Five years ago she formed the Coalition to Repeal the Eighth Amendment. I asked her about the strategy to win a campaign that had the odds stacked against it.

Define victory: what did winning look like for the Repeal the Eighth campaign?

'Winning this campaign was about repealing the amendment in its entirety and giving all women of Ireland the right to choice when it comes to abortions. But before we even won the referendum, we had to persuade the government to hold a referendum in the first place.'

This was a referendum campaign, where the public got to make the final decision. The law they were fighting was steeped in referendums. It came to fruition as a result of a referendum in 1983 and three further votes were held subsequently, allowing women to travel in and out of Ireland to have an abortion, authorising the giving of information about abortion services overseas and permitting abortions when doctors felt a woman's life may be at risk from pregnancy complications or suicide.

The 2018 referendum question asked whether the public wanted to remove the Eighth Amendment, which gives equal right to life to the mother and the unborn, and replace it with wording that would allow politicians to set Ireland's abortion laws in the future.

'We had to convince the parties they had to do the referendum in the first place. So we set up an organisation to repeal the Eighth Amendment in 2016. The idea was to bring all the organisations campaigning about this together and fight in a concerted way. The issue was contentious and difficult – it looked insoluble. And so we had to be extremely strategic so that our resources weren't going all over the place. We brought together human rights organisations, trades unions, women's rights groups, pro-choice campaigns. We started with twelve and ended up with just over a hundred.

'We did everything we could to secure a referendum: political lobbying, public awareness messaging, direct action. So the campaign for Repeal the Eighth started way back then. The network was vital – when the referendum was called, we were already at seventy to eighty members. Our strategy was to prepare. So by the time it was called we would be referendum-ready.'

What was the theory of change?

One of the common reasons cited in the struggle to Repeal the Eighth was that in a deeply Catholic country, where abortion had been stigmatised, the subject of abortion was taboo and rarely discussed. So those who were against abortion stayed stuck in their views and were never challenged with alternative ideas. In order to win the campaign, the stigma around abortion needed to be lifted and to do that, people needed to be able to talk about it. The theory of change was essentially to enable conversations, to give people the ability to tell their stories of the devastating impact of the Eighth Amendment.

'The key to the success was that foundations were laid back a long way. The referendum was only a ten-week period, but we had been doing focus-group research for three to four years. We knew people wanted to talk but didn't like the words "abortion" or "choice". They were triggering. So we approached these conversations carefully and very prepared.'

Identify and understand your decision-maker

This was a referendum campaign so the decision-makers were anyone of a voting age. Dialogue was the main barrier standing between those who would vote 'No' and those who were undecided. Campaign groups quickly realised that you just needed to have one conversation with people about the personal impact that the Eighth Amendment has had, and with this decades-long law, most people were likely to know at least one person affected.

'We needed to hit the right tone: respecting the others' point of view, offering opinions but not imposing them. When you're coming at an issue from two different sides, you take a moderate approach. You gain nothing by shouting; the sensible part of you has to come out. And you need to have something real to say. We were saying, "This isn't about right or wrong, it's about a reality." We took it out of a moral arena and moved it to a health issue. Away from the foetus to the woman.'

While this law was in place, women weren't able to have abortions even in the cases of rape or fatal foetal abnormalities. The fact that women were travelling all the way to England to go through the procedure meant they could not go straight home and rest afterwards, presenting a risk to their health in cases of losing consciousness or haemorrhage.

'We were saying that this law was putting women's lives at risk and that's how we got our message through. There is a place for the shouting and passion – it's how you get people mobilised. But when you need people to commit to vote, they weren't going to vote for themselves, the vast majority weren't thinking of themselves, so you had to motivate them to vote. It's about listening as much as it's about talking.

'Social media is important but doesn't beat being on the ground and having actual conversations. Asking the voter, what are your fears and reservations? We want to listen. And Ireland really listens to radio so we focused a lot of our efforts on getting our message there.'

Develop and articulate your campaign message to convince them

The campaign messaging was simple; while the No campaign focused on religion and the right to life, the Yes campaign gave a voice to the negative reality the Eighth Amendment had created in the country over thirty-five years. The trips to England to seek abortions, the rushed trips back that caused medical problems and sometimes deaths. The fear of taking an unregulated pill. These were all stories, spoken first-hand, that would stay with you all the way to the ballot box. It was the personal stories highlighted in the media which influenced 43% of the vote, according to an RTÉ exit poll.

And they did it strategically, creating a central story lab, with a pool of first-person stories of the difficulties of denying someone an abortion, which all the groups had access to. It meant that all the really powerful stories and people's experiences were collated in one place for easy access, lifting the output of everyone's messaging. That was a game-changer. People don't trust politicians or the media or the Church. But they trust doctors and professionals and women who have had abortions and were speaking from their heart.

Identify key supporters

The campaign would not have won without the support of political parties, civil society organisations, members of the public who would volunteer hours, days, months to the campaign and – most crucially – the women who had stories to tell. These weren't easy to get, it's a big ask for someone to speak of a deeply personal experience like abortion, but it was crucial in winning.

'The turnout on the day was incredible. We had a population ready for change. Imposing your views never works, people needed to express their own views, and many had changed their minds. It was a feeling of immense relief to know that this huge obstacle to women's freedom would be lifted. It was simply gone.

'There was a great sense of joy. We were celebrating a freedom. A coming of age of a country. And a deep sense of satisfaction that people who had been brainwashed were now choosing truth and honesty. And we were very, very, very tired!'

*

The five steps

It's all very well having lots of passion for an issue you want to work on, but where do you channel that energy, where to start? There have been so many campaigns that I've wanted to start over the years after having a really energising conversation about an issue, or watching something awful happen in the news; I realised something needed to change but I didn't take that first step. Because I wasn't sure what that first step should be. Not knowing where to start or what to do next is very human, it's a feeling of something being so big that you just freeze and do nothing. It happens to even the most seasoned campaigner – which is why I've broken it down into five major steps to make it easier for you to get started and know what you should be thinking about next.

The steps are important as they feed into each other – some of the campaign mistakes I've seen and made myself have been from not getting the campaign foundations right, like going straight into influencing the decision-maker before the messaging was right. Years ago I worked on a campaign with a Somali woman living in Camden, to get the drug *khat* banned in the UK. *Khat* is a plant that is chewed to release a natural stimulant. Its effects include alertness, speeding up of the user's mind and body, and also sometimes anxiety and aggression. It's also highly addictive and predominantly used by the men of the Somali community. But when I met Zeinab she told me that because of the addictive and aggressive nature of the drug, women were bearing the brunt of these side effects. We set about getting this law changed, but wanted to start by engaging her community in Camden. We decided to organise an event and spent months planning it, securing a community hall, making flyers, inviting the local residents as well as politicians that we wanted to influence, and the press. When it came to the day, we were disappointed that only a handful of people turned up. Five at most. It was a disheartening start and quite honestly, stressful. There's something excruciating about holding an event and no one turning up. Looking back, we made a key mistake: we hadn't built up any kind of support for the campaign, so people had no connection or understanding of what we were doing. They didn't know why it was important that they came and they hadn't had any time to really engage with the issue. We just invited them to an event out of the blue and expected sheer curiosity to make them turn up in large numbers. I created a lot of anxiety and stress for myself by trying to do many of the steps at once (gathering support, creating awareness, influencing the decision-maker). At the time it felt like such a waste of my energy and work and put me off grassroots campaigning for a while. Failure is hard, but we have to go through these mistakes so that we learn from them (I will talk about this later). By putting together these steps I'm hoping you'll avoid the obvious ones, giving you room to make your own!

Step One: What Gets You Mad? (or, What Is Your Ask?)

'The most courageous act is still to think for yourself. Aloud.'

— Coco Chanel

If you're like me, a lot of things put a bee in your bonnet. So the first challenge is picking something, of all the things that wind you up, to focus on. The next challenge is turning it from a mad rant into something specific.

Be SMART

I often meet people who want to campaign; they're really passionate about climate change, women's rights or racial justice, but they get overwhelmed by the scale of the issue. Stopping racism in an industry or trying to stop climate change feels like an impossible task so they freeze. They don't do anything. Campaigning is daunting, and impossible, unless you break down what you want to do into achievable tasks, by making your ask 'SMART'.

- Specific
- Measurable
- Achievable
- Responsible
- Time-sensitive

To quote American philanthropist Elbert Hubbard: 'Many people fail in life, not for lack of ability or brains or even courage, but simply because they have never organised their energies around a goal.' The concept of a SMART goal originates from a management consultant, George T. Doran. The idea took off in almost every other sphere of life, because it's simple and it works.

You ideally want your campaign to be SMART to increase your chances of winning. Why? Because it makes your campaign goal tangible. This is important because you can then visualise what victory looks like, and this will motivate you – and one of the biggest challenges of campaigning is keeping motivated. Setting a goal means you instinctively think about the steps ahead of you, making you face the right direction, focusing your actions. Your mind is a powerful thing: if it believes in something, the actions, the actual doing, is easy. The power of goal-setting is greater than you realise.

I'll take two possible campaigns as an example of a SMART and a non-SMART ask:

1. Stop air pollution
2. A car-free day in London by the end of the year

Make it specific

Both of these campaigns are specific to a degree, but one is much more specific than the other. Air pollution is a big issue and difficult to grapple with; it's broad and you could approach solving it in different ways. The second ask narrows down the campaign to a specific goal. A car-free day in London isn't going to solve the problem of air pollution overnight, but it's the first step and starts the right conversations about the impact cities have on air pollution, the responsibility of the car industry, and the health of those living in the city. No campaign will ever be a silver bullet to a problem, no one will solve air pollution overnight, but it's important to take the steps toward eradicating it and so being specific is vital.

Is it measurable?

The campaign goal 'Stop air pollution' is very difficult to measure, as it specifies no particular reduction or time frame. The campaign goal of a car-free day in London is much more practical. Here, the ask is scaled down to a city where you can easily measure how many cars drive in the year. The problem with non-measurable campaign asks is that they can be demotivating. If you have a goal that is so big it's not measurable, you will never know when you're close to victory and never be able to celebrate reaching a milestone. And this is crucial to keeping up the passion and commitment for yourself and for your supporters.

Is it achievable?

Be realistic about your ask and don't set yourself up to fail. If your aim is to end air pollution, that's OK, but your ask should be achievable, otherwise what's the point? Keep your idealism, but without a realistic ask you won't make a difference. It will also impact whether people join your cause, whether allies work with you and ultimately whether you win. Supporters are less likely to jump on board if something doesn't seem realistic and achievable; they need to know that their support will have some value.

Stopping air pollution is the ideal, but calling for London to join cities like Bath, Reykjavík (Iceland), and La Rochelle (France) to hold a car-free day once a year to encourage drivers to use public transport is both tangible and has a precedent in other cities. It may be trickier for a city like London, but there's a difference between an unachievable ask and a hard ask. Many people said that Ireland would never vote for the right to abortion, because of the long Catholic history of the country – that just wasn't true. If there's one thing that my experience has taught me, it's that the impossible is always possible. By breaking the campaign down into stages, to first win the right to a referendum and then focus on getting the outcome they wanted, the audacious vision to repeal the Eighth gradually became achievable.

Who is responsible?

Another stumbling block to wanting to stop air pollution is that it's impossible to know who's responsible for the decision: the Department of Health, the Department of Transport, or the prime minister? The issue belongs to all and none. Your ask needs to identify a decision-maker so that they feel accountable. In the case of the second ask, the decision-maker would be the Mayor of London. We'll dig more into decision-makers later.

Is it time-sensitive?

There is nothing like urgency to get the public's attention, the media interested and build momentum. Campaigns can last a long time, but by creating a deadline, and explaining why, you can increase the likelihood of victory. Research your topic and think about when it would be too late to make this change, or if there is a particular date that would make this decision more significant or more newsworthy. Don't just pick any date, it needs to make sense, but by doing that, you're essentially giving the decision-maker a deadline to respond to you.

Tackling homelessness with SMART

I started working on homelessness issues during what felt like the peak of hatred towards people on benefits. While the government was busy making drastic changes to the benefits system, which had seriously negative consequences for people who were homeless or relied on benefits, TV programmes were making entertainment out of the poor. The Channel 4 programme *Benefits Street* created controversy and fuelled debate with its middle-class gaze on a street in Birmingham. At this time writer Owen

Jones wrote that the 'hatred of those on benefits is danger-
ously out of control'. As a campaigner on homelessness
issues, it seemed impossible to get the public on side when
both the media and government were determined to treat
the most vulnerable as subhuman. It would be unbelieva-
ble to think that a campaign about homelessness could
lead to front-page news and cause one of the most conservative members of the Conservative Party to back the
campaign. But that's what happened, and we did it with
SMART campaigning.

It started when a picture of 'homeless spikes' went
viral on Twitter. These metal spikes were pictured
outside a block of luxury flats in South London,
designed to stop homeless people from sleeping in the
doorway. There was immediate outrage online, many
calling the spikes inhumane and comparing them to
spikes used to stop pigeons landing on buildings. Tweets
like 'These anti-homeless studs are like the spikes they
use to keep pigeons off buildings. The destitute now
considered vermin' and 'Anti-homeless floor studs. So
much for community spirit' did the rounds. At the
height of a vicious narrative about homeless people this
was a step too far. It seemed like the prime opportunity
to mobilise this support from the public for homeless
people. I worked with Harriet, a mental health nurse
for North Camden Crisis Team whose work included

providing support for homeless people. She explained her reason for campaigning: 'As a mental health nurse in London I have all too often seen the result of isolating and mistreating our city's homeless. We should be offering practical and emotional support to help the most vulnerable get back on their feet. We should not be sending them the message that they are pests that need to be warded off.'

As soon as the spikes were spotted, the public rallied together and demanded their removal. Over 130,000 people signed Harriet's petition calling for both the developers of the property and for the Mayor of London, at the time Boris Johnson, to do better. The property was owned by a private company which could technically do what it wanted. But the pressure on the Mayor was making this a problem for the people of London. The media ran headlines in support of the campaign and blasting this faceless property company for their lack of response. Despite being called for comment by journalists, they kept quiet, which only created more distrust, and more support for the campaign. Soon Boris Johnson spoke out and said they needed to go. And these weren't the only spikes; it seemed they were a common deterrent used by property companies and pictures of spikes spotted around London started appearing on social media. Within days of Harriet's petition, spikes were spotted outside a branch of Tesco in central London.

The next day, a group of activists poured cement over them, forcing Tesco to have them removed hours later. It was then just a matter of keeping up the pressure. And then, within five days of the petition, one morning the spikes in Southwark were gone. With no statement or word from the developers who owned the building, they had disappeared overnight. Not only had the campaign won, but it had started an important discussion that was a long time coming, about attitudes to homelessness in the capital.

The campaign was SMART – it was specific, in that it wasn't trying to end all homelessness in one go. It was clearly measurable as the impact would be evident when the spikes were removed. It was a difficult ask, calling for this faceless company to remove something from their building when they had no incentive to. But the strategy, of mobilising the public mood and getting the Mayor involved, made it achievable. Who was responsible? While the property company was the main decision-maker, we knew that Boris Johnson would feel a degree of ownership over the issue. So targeting him with the campaign was a creative way of increasing that feeling of responsibility. And the fact that Harriet acted so fast in starting her petition, and then responded in real time to events as they quickly changed, created a time-sensitivity to the campaign that hadn't been there in the first place.

Your battleground

Whether you want to campaign to save your local library from closing down or to fight climate change, the campaigning principles will be the same. But the journey will be very different and you should think carefully about your battleground; how local, national or global you want your campaign to be.

Local

Campaigning on local issues can have the most direct impact on your life, and decision-makers are easier to access. It's worth noting that local campaigns don't always stay local; they can gain national attention, and point to a systemic problem.

In 2014 the New Era estate in East London celebrated saving their homes after a six-month-long campaign. Plans to hike up rents to market rates would have put families living on this housing estate out on the street; with most residents on low-income wages, they couldn't afford the crippling increase that was proposed. No one expected them to win, they were up against their new landlord, US property company Westbrook Partners, but the residents were prepared to do anything to keep their homes.

Within months of starting the campaign, resident Lindsay Garrett's petition went viral. Reminiscent of the 1980s miners' strike and the fight for equal pay by Ford factory workers in the 1960s, the campaign captured the country's imagination in telling the story of ninety-three 'Davids' versus a massive 'Goliath'. But unlike the former campaigns, New Era won in a matter of weeks, because their campaign was amplified nationally, and also globally, through the internet. The internet made solidarity and mobilisation bigger, faster and more powerful. The campaign was covered by press all over the world. At one point, even the Mayor of New York intervened, coming to the residents' defence.

Local issues are often an indicator that there is a wider problem, so just because your campaign is about your area, it doesn't mean it won't engage people around the world.

The key to any good campaign is smart and well-executed online and offline tactics and telling an incredible story. Lindsay's campaign captured the attention of the entire country, making national headlines, because it spoke to the problem of crippling rents and luxury housing pushing lower-income earners out of areas across the country.

National and global

Going wider and calling for change on a national or global scale can be quite scary, but as long as your campaign is SMART, there is no reason why it can't win. Make sure you have a good grasp of the issue and the people affected by the issue. If you don't have a connection to the issue personally, then ask yourself if you're the right person to be campaigning about this. If there is a good reason, then it's vital that you're in direct contact with people in that community so that you can speak with a strong understanding of the matter and also empower those with experiences of the problem to speak out.

For example, when Laura Coryton won her campaign for the government to commit to ending the tampon tax, she put her energies into another period-related problem: the sad fact that homeless women and trans men across the country have no free provision to sanitary care and will resort to anything from socks, plastic bags and napkins, to rags, shirts and cotton balls. These homeless people are at risk of toxic shock syndrome and other health-related issues if they can't access free and hygienic sanitary products. Laura started a new campaign aimed at persuading Procter and Gamble to provide sanitary products to homeless shelters across the UK. Laura was privileged enough to have never experienced homelessness, so as part of her planning of the campaign she reached out to shelters and homeless services to speak to women who had experienced this issue first-hand. She used her platform to amplify these women's voices and supported them in speaking to the media as part of her campaign.

Corporate

Stevie Wise ran the Sexist Surcharge campaign after finding out that high-street chemist Boots were charging more for razors aimed at women, which were identical to those aimed at men – except they were pink. Fed up with accepting the way companies were targeting and profiting from women, she ran a successful campaign that trended on Twitter, gathered thousands of signatures, involved her speaking on air to the media and eventually bagging a meeting with the Boots CEO. They agreed to change their pricing, as did their high-street rival Superdrug. Stevie proved that consumers have a lot of bargaining power.

It's not just governments that hold power; companies are sometimes the best target because they're not as used to being lobbied and, depending on the type of company, they're likely to care about their brand. If you do this, try to get in contact with people who work there: it can be a powerful message if employees of a corporation are backing a campaign against them, and could be the thing you need to tip toward victory.

Workplace

There are many unions set up to help employees advocate for better rights at work. If you're a member of a trade union, you should contact them to see if they can help with your problem at work first.

Campaigning at your workplace is an incredibly sensitive issue as it can put your job at risk. But at the same time, workplace issues are some of the most personal, which can affect us deeply. And creating change with your employer could have a huge impact for the rest of the workforce.

After the UK's national living wage rose to £7.20 in 2016, employees across Britain thought they would be better off. But some companies increased staff wages by making cuts in other places, like scrapping Sunday and bank holiday double pay and cutting pensions. I worked with a B&Q store manager, Kevin Smith (not his real name), who decided to start a petition to stop the company making these cuts, saying that it would hit junior staff hardest, some of whom had been in the company for over a decade. Worse still, he had been tasked to carry out the staff consultation ahead of these proposed cuts. 'As a manager it has been incredibly difficult conducting consultations with people that are set to lose thousands of pounds and telling them that if they don't sign by March 24th they will lose their job,' Kevin said at the time. He felt compelled to speak up but knew that if he did, he would risk his job. So he became a whistle-blower and campaigned under a fake name. His campaign drew wide support in Parliament and across the UK in the media. In his petition Kevin claimed that B&Q were forcing staff to sign a new contract (on threat of dismissal), which included the following changes:

- Removal of time-and-a-half pay for working Sundays
- Removal of summer and winter bonuses equating to 6% of annual salary
- Reduction of bank holiday rates from double pay to time-and-a-half pay
- Restructuring of allowances for working in high-cost-of-living areas of the UK

When national media interviewed Kevin, they did so behind screens so that he couldn't be identified. Fellow workers signed his campaign and spoke up with their experiences. B&Q disputed some of the campaigners' claims, but just a few months after starting the campaign the company conceded, offering workers affected by the cuts two years of compensation. To this day they don't know who Kevin Smith is.

There are lots of resources out there about speaking up at work; make sure you do your research and understand your rights before starting a campaign. Here are a couple of places to start:

www.acas.org.uk
Acas offers advice and information on a wide range of workplace issues to try and help employees and employers to solve their problems at work. You can either call them or use their online helpline.

www.citizensadvice.org.uk
Citizens Advice offer free, confidential information and advice to assist people with money, legal, consumer and employment problems.

The art of messaging

'Words – so innocent and powerless as they are, as standing in a dictionary, how potent for good and evil they become in the hands of one who knows how to combine them.'

— Nathaniel Hawthorne

I love words and one thing I love about campaigning is how it gives power to language like nothing else. This has been one of the most empowering and liberating things I've learned in my years of campaigning, because words are free for everyone to use, and if you use them well, they become more powerful than power and privilege itself.

'My name is Greta Thunberg. I am fifteen years old. I am from Sweden. I speak on behalf of Climate Justice Now. Many people say that Sweden is just a small country and it doesn't matter what we do. But I've learned you are never too small to make a difference. And if a few children can get headlines all over the world just by not going to school, then imagine what we could all do together if we really wanted to.

'But to do that, we have to speak clearly, no matter how uncomfortable that may be. You only speak of green eternal economic growth because you are too scared of being unpopular. You only talk about moving forward with the same bad ideas that got us into this mess, even when the only sensible thing to do is pull the emergency brake. You are not mature enough to tell it like it is. Even that burden you leave to us children. But I don't care about being popular. I care about climate justice and the living planet. Our civilisation is being sacrificed for the opportunity of a very small number of people to continue making enormous amounts of money. Our biosphere is being sacrificed so that rich people in countries like mine can live in luxury. It is the sufferings of the many which pay for the luxuries of the few.'

This was the beginning of a speech delivered by Greta Thunberg at a UN climate conference, to a roomful of some of the most powerful leaders in the world. This speech sparked a wildfire, with children in more than a hundred countries striking (literally striking from school!) every Friday to protest and demand their governments take urgent action on climate.

Climate change is an issue that has been tackled in various ways for decades. Activists who know and understand the issue have struggled to communicate the issue to the wider public. Every year, as the weather dramatically changes, natural disasters increase and scientists warn of the threat looming, public consciousness lies in a deep sleep. So what was it about Greta's words that woke people up with such a start? The answer is quite simple – the messaging and framing was on point.

Why it's important to get your message right

Messaging is important because it is the way you will change people's minds. You might think it's obvious why you are calling for change but we all have different lived experiences, so what is obvious and a no-brainer for one person can be difficult to understand for the next.

A common pitfall is to collect all of the facts and statistics about a particular issue and bombard your audience with them in an attempt to convince them to support you. But people remember stories, not statistics. Numbers are forgettable because they are geared to the logical left side of your brain. Research has shown that numbers don't easily stick in the long-term memory of most people.

This doesn't mean facts and figures shouldn't be used, but they need to be part of a more engaging message. The London School of Business found that when people hear statistics alone, they retain only 5% to 10% of what they hear. When the statistic is coupled with a picture related to it, retention jumps to 25% – a good increase compared to statistics alone, but probably not enough to compel others to make long-lasting changes. When stories are used to convey that same information, retention jumps to a remarkable 65% to 70%. That's right, I just used statistics to make a point about their limitations. Go figure.

If you want to create a deeper and quicker level of trust with others, you need to use stories. Greta's speech wasn't filled with the statistics and scientific evidence of the threat we face with climate change. It was a story of a young person standing up to the adults and telling them to grow up. There's one part of her speech that has stayed with me, that I find unsettling and effective: 'You are not mature enough to tell it like it is. Even that burden you leave to us children.' You can feel the weight of her disappointment. Greta's words delivered the impact that endless academic reports never could. That's how you change minds.

The Syrian refugee crisis

The scientific journal entitled *Proceedings of the National Academy of Sciences of the United States* (PNAS) published a paper on the power of images during a humanitarian crisis. In 2015 as the Syrian war intensified, families were fleeing to Europe in desperation to save their lives. According to the UN, by July of that year the conflict in Syria had driven more than 4 million people – a sixth of the population – to seek sanctuary in neighbouring countries, making it the largest refugee crisis for a quarter of a century. The conflict had killed more than 220,000 people. The UN were calling on international communities to step up and offer these refugees sanctuary, but most of Europe, the USA and Canada remained closed and it seemed impossible to sway both public and political opinion to do more. The PNAS report said, 'we cannot assume that the statistics of mass human crises will capture our attention or move us to take action, no matter how large the numbers. The data that we present show that the world was basically asleep as the body count in the Syrian war rose steadily into the hundreds of thousands.'

But then something happened on 2nd September 2015 that shook the world. Alan Kurdi, a three-year-old boy, drowned in the Mediterranean Sea as his family were fleeing Syria. A picture of his little body washed up on shore went viral. That heart-breaking picture stopped the UK in its tracks. Suddenly, it seemed, people understood the human cost of the political situation. It led to a mass demonstration and the #RefugeesWelcome campaign and petition, which included the public, celebrities and politicians across the UK, tweeting the hashtag with a picture holding the words 'Refugees Welcome' and urging David Cameron, the prime minister at the time, to accept more Syrian refugees into the UK. One photograph turned something we all knew was happening, but to people from a place that was little known and far away, into a gut-wrenching tragedy that demanded immediate action. Even the *Sun*, which just months before had published a column describing the refugees as 'cockroaches', now put 'For Aylan' (as his name was initially reported) on its front page and demanded that the government provide places for 3,000 orphans. The pressure worked – David Cameron announced that the UK would accept 20,000 Syrian refugees by 2020.

But this is also an astonishingly vivid demonstration of the inadequacy of statistics to move our moral sentiments when compared with the power of pictures that bring to life stories, and which affect us in ways that reasoning just can't. Story is how religions gain followers. Story is the most powerful weapon you will have as a campaigner. One single death in a refugee family moved a nation to whom 200,000 deaths and 11 million refugees had remained merely statistics.

Messaging is the heart of your campaign – everything should start and end with your messaging. Once you have it, you need to repeat it over and over again. US Republican strategist Frank Luntz said, 'There's a simple rule: you say it again, and you say it again, and you say it again, and you say it again, and you say it again, and then again and again and again and again, and about the time that you're absolutely sick of saying it is about the time that your target audience has heard it for the first time.' The idea is that a message has to be seen multiple times before a person a) notices and b) responds favourably. This has been used in advertising to sell products. It's the same with messaging – you're selling something, even if it's an idea or point of view. It's tempting when you think something isn't working to drop it and try a different tack. But with messaging, you have to stick with it if it is going to have any chance of success.

Framing your message

DON'T THINK OF AN ELEPHANT!

Chances are you now have an image of an elephant in your head. George Lakoff, a cognitive linguist, used this to demonstrate that almost all thought is automatic and unconscious. Our brains process information so quickly, we have little control of the things that pop into our minds when we observe things or receive messages. Political operators and advertisers know this very well and will use this to get across their message. Our brains make mental shortcuts to help us organise the information we receive; these shortcuts and associations are known as 'frames'.

Here's an example of framing. What sounds scarier to you, global warming or climate change? Conservatives know that 'climate change' sounds less scary than 'global warming'. We know this because a leaked memo shows the aforementioned Frank Luntz advising George W. Bush to use the term 'climate change':

> It's time for us to start talking about 'climate change' instead of 'global warming' . . . As one focus group participant noted, climate change 'sounds like you're going from Pittsburgh to Fort Lauderdale.' While global warming has catastrophic connotations attached to it, climate change suggests a more controllable and less emotional challenge.

This is framing: you take the same issue – the planet's rising temperature – and communicate that issue in a way that persuades people you have the best ideas, approach, whatever.

Are you using the same language as those who hold the opposite view to your own? If so, you might be using a frame that serves their interest and not yours.

How to come up with a strong message

> 'I've learned that people will forget what you said, people will forget what you did, but people will never forget how you made them feel.'

> — Maya Angelou

Hollywood has nailed this. Every film and TV drama is carefully created to impact you in very specific ways, your feelings dictated by the writers and directors. Good storytelling is an art and draws in audiences. Campaign messaging is a bit like that and some of the best movements have tapped into classic storylines to engage their supporters and influence their decision-maker. A strong campaign narrative involves:

1. *A hero/protagonist*
   The protagonist or hero is you. And the hero can also be the supporter. How can you make them feel as though their help will save the day? Or the decision-maker; can you frame your campaign to make them feel that they could literally be the hero of this story?

2. *Emotion*
   Does this story elicit empathy? Is there someone that you feel for? Does it produce outrage, because

there is a burning injustice? Or hope, because this is a story of empowerment? Pinpoint the main emotion you want to channel from your supporters and use that to create your tone.

3. *A beginning, middle and end*
   Take the supporter on a journey. Once they have joined, tell them what's coming and always remind them of what the hero is trying to achieve. Make sure they know where they are in that journey.

4. *Conflict*
   This might be somebody who wants something badly and is having difficulty getting it. Or perhaps something very bad is about to happen and we need to stop it. Without conflict, there's no plot or story worth telling. This is key to your narrative. Ask yourself, who is the conflict between? What does it say about the values of those people? Is it like another familiar conflict that you can remind people of (like the story of David vs Goliath)?

5. *Something that's at stake*
   Why is this so important? Something bad will happen if the hero doesn't win. What is that? Who will win or lose, and what will the impact of that be? This is

one of the most compelling parts to your story, along
with the conflict, because it helps you to create a
sense of urgency and keeps the supporters on board.

Approach your campaign message in the same way as
writing a story. In order to persuade the audience, you
need to have them hooked. You need a hero or a protagonist and a clear path to victory. You can (subtly) present
the people in your campaign as characters in a story, in
pursuit of a goal that expresses their values.

**When we hear stories based on these patterns
they are more akin to *remembering* rather than
learning something new. Which makes it a
powerful messaging technique.**

Give it weight

You need facts and figures – but just don't overdo it.
You need logic; statistics back up the storytelling element
and back up your points with evidence. However, with
most issues there are complex policies and a ton of
jargon that is useful for you to be familiar with, but
which doesn't need to be communicated to all of your
audience. At the same time, people want to know the
basics, especially if it gives the issue legitimacy, so don't

completely keep the detail away from them, just don't overwhelm them with it.

Spend some time on your campaign researching what's already out there and what information you need to find for yourself. Articulating figures is an art; don't confuse people with complicated numbers, try to make the stats as easy to understand as possible. For example:

- Rather than '82%', say, 'More than 80%'
- Don't say '67%', say, 'Two-thirds'
- Not '95 years ago', say, 'Almost one hundred years ago'
- Instead of '6,300 people', say, 'More than 6,000 people'

Messaging workshop

With a few people, brainstorm the following questions:

1. How do you want people to feel?
2. What are the facts and is there evidence?
3. How do you want people to think about the issue when you frame it? Think carefully about which words you want to use.
4. Who is the hero and who is the villain in your story?
5. What's at stake? What will happen if this doesn't go the way the hero wants?

6. What can people do to help the hero win?
7. Now, using your notes, boil your message down to one paragraph, summing up the story and eliciting the feelings you want your audience to feel.
8. What's the image that conveys this message? It doesn't matter if this doesn't already exist; brainstorm the kind of compelling image you need to tell your story.

And when that's done, test it!

Testing your message

Don't take it as a given that after that work, your message is perfect. Ask at least ten people what they think and feel when they read your message. But don't just ask the ones who already agree with you. Find people who know nothing about the issue, and people who are opposed, and take notes on what they say. It doesn't mean you should change the message to suit ten different people, but if there are common themes coming up, it will start to give you an idea of what works and what doesn't. And practise putting across your message in social settings where you're competing for attention; if you had to explain the campaign at a noisy family dinner in two minutes or in a busy pub to a rowdy group of friends, would the message still land? It needs to cut through in these settings so that you have stress-tested it for the extremely distracted world we're all living in.

Spread your message

After you have found the right message, internalise it, learn it. You should be able to recite it quickly, with passion. And then start spreading it. As the recurring element of your campaign, you should include your message in everything you do.

Never tire of repeating it again and again. It can feel a bit silly when you first start doing this but trust me, this is how you get people to remember. Repeat the same message over and over again until you are sick of saying it – that's when people have started listening.

Step Two: Friends, Foes, Allies and Lizards

'We can learn to see each other and see ourselves in each other and recognize that human beings are more alike than we are unalike.'

— Maya Angelou

Luke felt helpless. He'd just found out that his friend Brian was in trouble and he wanted to help but didn't know how.

Luke grew up in Wolverhampton and met his best friend Brian at school. Brian had been abandoned in Zimbabwe until he was six when he was fostered by a British family and taken to Botswana. At the age of fifteen, the family adopted him and brought Brian to the UK, which became his home. Only when Brian made his university application did he discover that he didn't have the correct immigration status due to a Home Office error. His application to become a British citizen by naturalisation had been incorrectly rejected at the time of arriving and he had only been granted limited leave to remain in the UK. That meant that when applying to study chemistry at Oxford, the university turned him down due to his immigration status.

Luke had watched Brian study hard for the three A*s and an A that had earned him a place on Oxford's renowned course. That place, and his future, was now at risk because of a Home Office error. For people in Brian's shoes, it's difficult to speak up. But knowing that his friend could lose everything, and that he could lose his friend, Luke couldn't stay quiet – he started to campaign.

In just a week, over 100,000 people backed the campaign and journalists from every major outlet got in touch to tell Brian's story – the story was splashed on just about every national TV channel, radio station and newspaper you can think of. Celebrities started to tweet. And then came support from politicians across the political spectrum. Influential people like the Chief Whip, Gavin Williamson, said he planned to raise this directly with the Home Secretary. And the Police and Crime Commissioner in Brian's area asked to meet with Brian, tweeting afterwards to urge the Home Office to 'see sense'.

Brian felt less alone but he was still scared. He told the *Guardian*, 'I'm not legally allowed to work, so I assume I would be deported to Africa, I don't know anyone there.

I'd have to start again. This is the most important thing to me right now. Everyone I know and love lives here.'

Luke is the person I mentioned at the start of this book, who said that before he spoke up, his view was that campaigners were tree-huggers. He and his mate Brian were just a couple of working-class kids from the Midlands who thought no one would listen to them, especially not the Home Office – which can come across as one of the more intimidating government departments. But by sticking his neck out, Luke proved to everyone, including himself, that they couldn't be ignored. Finally, the Home Office conceded. And now Brian is studying at Oxford University.

Decision-makers ... are not all lizards

They may give you the heebie-jeebies and drive you absolutely bananas, but the more we paint the decision-maker as a lizard, as a repellent creature that devours animals in their lairs, the further we place ourselves from getting to campaign victory. The moment I realised this, and changed my approach to campaigning, I made a lot more progress and had a nicer time while I did it. Don't get me wrong, it's fun to dehumanise someone who is powerful and abusing that power for their own benefit. I get it, I agree. But it doesn't help you, and that's all I'm really interested in. It's common behaviour to position yourself in opposition to your decision-maker so much that you forget they're human. They become the enemy because they're standing between you and your goal, and depending on what you're campaigning about, they are either a part of the problem or maintaining the problem. Lots of campaigners are argumentative, indignant people by nature (hi!) and when you're passionate and argumentative, you can have a tendency to dehumanise those that don't agree with you. To be completely honest with you I find this very hard. I spent half my life feeling explicitly ignored and judged as unimportant by those in power. Growing up in the Midlands, harassed on a daily basis, my family worked hard to have the authorities take us seriously. We often felt either ignored or patronised. So I find it difficult to keep my patience with those in power. I'm the first to admit that I probably have a chip or two on my shoulder, and it's hard to brush these off because those feelings go deep and are rooted within a wider problem in society, namely, a problem of institutions systematically ignoring the most marginal or vulnerable. But I, and you, also want to win. And the decision-maker is the person who is going to help us win – by coming on board. So take a deep breath, unclench those teeth, and start trying to understand them.

To create change, you have to influence the right people who make the decisions. I often see people get the decision-maker wrong, and you have no chance of winning the campaign if you're not talking to the right person – it's wasted time and energy. Believe it or not the prime minister is the most common decision-maker people choose when they're campaigning, and although the PM is at the highest level of decision-making in the country, they a) won't necessarily be the right person to make the change and b) are very, very busy. So by getting more specific with the person you target, your chances of victory increase dramatically. Do some research and find the specific person or department responsible for making the decision. They could be a councillor, an MP, a police chief, a minister, a newspaper editor, a CEO of a company, the chair of a board.

Who's in charge? Power-mapping

Power-mapping is a useful exercise to understand everyone involved in the world of your campaign, how influential they are and eventually how you'll win over the decision-maker. You can also use this exercise when your campaign has come to a standstill and the decision-maker isn't engaging at all. Map out who's who and see if you can pivot your campaign to another decision-maker. I'll come back to this strategy later.

Here's an example of a power map for Brian and Luke:

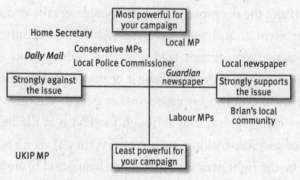

This is a helpful exercise to understand where to put your time and energy. For example, a UKIP MP would likely be against this campaign but they are the least influential so it's not worth your energy to engage them. Conservative MPs are naturally more powerful than Labour MPs when it's a Conservative government making the decision. But the Labour MPs still have some power: they can use their platform in Parliament to get the campaign noticed. And while the *Daily Mail* and the *Guardian* are both national newspapers and widely read by influential people, the *Mail*'s traditional stance on immigration makes their potential support of the campaign quite valuable; the government may think twice about holding a position seemingly more extreme than the extremely conservative *Daily Mail*.

Understand the decision-maker

In Luke and Brian's case, the decision-maker was the Home Office. The Home Office are a tough opponent to come up against; they're a national government department and any public decision they make will garner media attention and they know that – they have a lot at stake too.

First of all, as I said earlier, remember that the eventual decision-maker is human. They think, feel, sleep, eat, breathe just like you. It can be hard not to demonise them, especially if you're campaigning about something very personal and emotional. But demonising them won't help your campaign. Campaigning is a bit like negotiating; you need to form some element of trust with the person you're trying to convince. Start by understanding them.

Who are they? What do they read and listen to? OK, so unless you're full-on stalking (not something I recommend), then some of this might be hard to find out. But you can take a guess at which news channels and papers they're likely to consume. This will help you to know which magazines, newspapers, programmes to target when you're trying to get press – one way of getting your message into their ear.

Who are the people close to them, who are they influenced by? Do they have a board? CEOs have to report regularly to their boards, and are held accountable by them. Getting access to the board will give you a great influencing advantage. Does the decision-maker have a spouse in the public eye? In 2013 when we were campaigning to get the Education Secretary, Michael Gove, to address female genital mutilation in schools, we panicked when his wife, *Times* columnist Sarah Vine, wrote a column ridiculing the campaign. But then we stopped and realised we should be celebrating – it dawned on us that if she was writing about the campaign then the two of them must be discussing it, meaning Gove was aware of the campaign even though up until this point we had received nothing but radio silence from his department. Even though we hadn't heard a word from Gove's team, the image of the two of them discussing the campaign at the dinner table felt like success, or at least a step in the right direction.

With Brian's case, the Home Office weren't budging,

but once politicians in the Conservative Party started to speak up, and once the Police and Crime Commissioner had come on board, we knew that the campaign was getting somewhere. Both had a great deal of influence over the Home Secretary: a Conservative Home Secretary is more likely to listen to Members of Parliament in their own party and they are more likely to listen to the police force, which forms part of their remit. It is also quite unusual for someone in the police force to speak publicly about a campaign, so this was another plus, and the media cottoned onto that.

Your mission is for the decision-maker to know the following:

- Your name
- What you want
- That you aren't going anywhere fast

Politicians – friends or foes?

Like members of the public, MPs are a mixed bag. I've worked with politicians who treated me like a piece of furniture in the room: ignored, useful at times, but absolutely no need for eye contact, never mind a please or thank you. And I've worked with politicians who were and are so dedicated to the role of representing their area, and so passionate about that public service they have been elected to carry out, that they are some of the most inspiring campaigners I have worked with. So it would be a huge mistake to make broad assumptions before you meet them.

Whether your local Member of Parliament is your ultimate decision-maker or not, you should lobby them. Because even if they can't change things for you, they will be able to advocate on your behalf if you get them on side.

So what does your MP do?

Everyone has an MP. Even if you're not old enough to vote, your MP is elected by the people in your area to represent your views. Their role is to serve the community they live in, by representing your views in Parliament.

MPs differ in terms of how good they are with their constituents (you): some are very accessible and want to hear more from you and with others you might struggle to hear back. But you should try – and don't give up if it's proving difficult; it doesn't mean they're not interested, so persist!

What can your MP do for you?

If they're good, getting an influential person like an MP on side can really help your campaign. Backbench MPs (who don't have a role that restricts what they can and can't say publicly) can be incredibly influential campaigners because they have a platform to speak on, and tools at their disposal to create change. Here are a few things they can do, but the list goes on, depending on their experience and role in their party:

- They can publicly support your campaign, giving it some legitimacy.
- They can ask a question of a government minister (including the prime minister) in the House of Commons.
- They vote on bills, so if your issue is being debated in a bill in Parliament, you can convince them to vote the way you want.
- They can table a private members' bill – bills introduced by MPs or members of the House of Lords

who are not government ministers. They don't often pass but are a good way to get a debate in Parliament.

- They can table an early day motion – these are a bit like a petition started by MPs that expresses a statement that other MPs can sign and support. They're a way to draw attention to an issue, and effective if you can demonstrate cross-party support.
- They can request meetings with government officials on your behalf.
- They can write to companies, requesting meetings on your behalf.

But first, you need to convince them to support you.

How to get your MP on board

- If you don't know who your MP is, look them up online. Use the Parliament website (www.parliament.uk /mps-lords-and-offices/mps/) to search your postcode.
- Once you know who they are, do some research on them (online or asking around in your community). Find out what their big issues of concern are; do they align with your campaign? If so, write to them and tell them.
- MPs hold something called 'MP surgeries' usually on Fridays in their constituency. These are a bit like

open-door appointments where you can just turn up and wait for your time with the MP. Go prepared, take your research and be clear about what you want them to do. Find out when the next surgery is being held by looking on their website, or calling their office.

- For MPs you need more than your crafted message that persuades through storytelling. Make the case for why this is an important issue with evidence too, do the research and have some statistics or facts to back your argument up. If you can, find out how many more people are affected by the same issue.

- Give them a reason to support you. Does your message align with their values or something they are on record as having said? Maybe it would be good for their profile because you'll secure some media coverage of their support. Or demonstrate the number of people who support this issue with a petition.

- Go to them with an ask – what do you want them to do? Whether it's having a photo taken with you so that you can publicise their support, or asking a question for you in Parliament, give them some direction so that you know when you walk away that you've got what you need.

- Don't stop trying. They might not listen to you right away, but once your campaign starts to grow, go back and tell your MP how many supporters you have, the media coverage you have achieved and who else is supporting you. I've seen many MPs engage with a campaigner once they find out that over a thousand people are backing them.

Elections

If there is an election happening in your area, this is the best time to engage both the current and prospective candidates. During the period in the run-up to the election, known as purdah, big policy decisions and announcements are put on hold. And though the government can't make any decisions during this period, politicians are out there trying to win your vote. Take advantage of that and get your campaign on their agenda.

Although politicians can no longer act as decision-makers during this time, they can become influential spokespeople for campaigns. Do some research on which candidates are talking about your issue and get in touch. Politicians are professional campaigners and can really help you get your campaign out there, and win. This is what Caroline Criado-Perez did when she campaigned to get women represented on banknotes. She enlisted the support of female MPs like Stella Creasy who came out in support and helped her win.

During a pre-election period, party candidates will be especially keen to support local campaigners. Find out about local hustings in your area and go along to ask the candidates if they can support your campaign and ask what they will do to help.

They're not all the same . . .

The Speaker of the House of Commons has made waves in the media since he took his role. John Bercow is the first Speaker not to wear traditional court robes while presiding over the House of Commons; he made history when he allowed young people to be the first non-MPs ever to sit and debate in the Commons and has time and again shaped rules to make Parliament more open and inclusive. I first came across him as the Conservative MP for Buckingham who was a campaigning force for autism care, speaking from the experience of a father with an autistic child. His refusal to bow to party politics was inspiring; he seemed to care far more about getting things done than doing what was expected of him by the party machine. MPs get a bad rap but there are many out there who are incredible campaigners and advocates of people power. I spoke to John Bercow about the importance of getting your voice heard, and as the complete expert in Parliamentary process, exactly how you should do it.

'I cannot overstate the importance of people taking at least some interest in politics. It affects every aspect of our lives, be it through the education of our children, the health and social care of our parents, to how much tax we pay and the upkeep of our roads, etc. Politics does matter. Even if you are not that interested, I would ask you to allocate a part of your head space – at least to share a fraction of your thinking time – to politics, because it will affect your life.'

He's right. Even if you are put off by the idea of politics, it will affect your everyday life, and the more of us that are involved, the healthier and more effective politics will be.

To most people the Speaker is familiar as the person chairing proceedings in the House of Commons Chamber – he decides who shall speak in the House and maintains discipline with the refrain 'Order! Order!' Yes, I'm sure we've all become accustomed to that booming voice now, after the hours of Brexit news stories that have dominated our TV screens. You don't have to look far for a John Bercow meme, but his role is actually very influential for a campaigner.

'The Speaker must grapple with all the competing demands: the rights of backbenchers when the government has a (perhaps large) majority, the pressures on time – both for debate and questioning of the executive – the concerns of the official opposition and the smaller parties, and how to exercise the extensive powers given to him by the House. For example, whether to allow urgent questions and emergency debates and what amendments to select for debate on the report stages of bills.'

So what John Bercow is saying, is that the Speaker has the power to shape what is debated in the Commons, and so what gets on the political agenda. And as an MP and Speaker of the House, he says the best way to get your issue on the Westminster map is working with your MP.

He continues with this advice: 'I would get to know your local MP and explain to him or her what the issue is, and why you think it's important they should campaign for or against it. There are several ways you can do this – including attending the MP's regular surgery in your constituency, or by writing a letter or email. Alternatively, you could start a petition. If a petition receives 10,000 signatures, the government will respond. At 100,000 signatures, the petition will be considered for a debate in Parliament.' One caveat that I will add to that advice is that those numbers can feel quite intimidating to a person wanting to campaign but without a network of thousands to share their petition with. So don't let that put you off; it's just one of *many* mechanisms to getting your issue heard in Parliament.

And it works; petitions have made MPs stop in their

tracks. In 2017, a Westminster Hall debate over whether US President Donald Trump should be given a state visit to the UK was triggered by two petitions – one against, which received 1.85 million signatures. The other petition in favour of Mr Trump's visit attracted 311,000 signatures. Protests took place in central London as MPs clashed over the issue in Parliament. It could be argued that the petition against the visit had a contributory effect in deterring the government from inviting the president to visit the UK straight away.

And in 2013, MPs ruled out possible UK military action against Syrian President Assad's government to deter the use of chemical weapons. The then prime minister, David Cameron, who had recalled Parliament to decide whether the UK should join US-led strikes, said he would respect the defeat of the government motion. This followed the then Labour Party leader Ed Miliband's decision not to back the government. Mr Miliband claimed the Commons had spoken 'for the people of Britain' who 'want us to learn the lessons of Iraq'.

Allies

'United we stand, divided we fall' is a popular quote within unions for a reason. Change may start with one person but it rarely, if ever, has been achieved with just one.

When I was growing up in the Midlands, in a village that was 99% white working class, as the family running a newsagent's shop, we were often the target of abuse. This was mostly from the same gang of boys and their dads who didn't like the idea of the local newsagent's being run by an Indian family – the imbalance of power made them uneasy. My parents could refuse to serve them when they were illegally buying alcohol underage or throw them out of the shop when they were abusive. If you are a shopkeeper, you'll know that the other shops in your area are your direct competition; you are not natural allies. You keep an eye on how much the other shop is charging for milk and eggs so that your prices can stay competitive. If one of the shops gets an ATM installed, you know that's bad news for you and the rest because it will attract your customers. You naturally curse them, hoping that the ATM breaks on day one.

When my dad was struggling to get the police to take the racial abuse and harassment seriously, he formed an unlikely alliance with the other corner shops in the village. By forming a group they were able to wield more power with the police. They began meeting fortnightly, as a group of shopkeepers, to swap notes on the latest gang incident and how the police had responded. Eventually two things happened: the police heard about these regular meetups and started to join the shopkeepers at their meetings, taking action on their complaints and monitoring the gang behaviour, and the shopkeepers set up an alert network. If an incident had happened in one shop, that shopkeeper would alert the next, setting off a domino effect of phone calls around the village that would stop the gangs from hitting every shop. Today you might have a WhatsApp group. Sometimes, working with the so-called 'competition' is how you get things done.

Stories of unlikely alliances are inspiring because they're about putting egos aside for a greater good and about many small Davids coming together to defeat a giant Goliath – the odds are against them but together they are stronger.

Lesbians and gays support the miners

In 1984 two minority groups, who seemed to be so far apart in their beliefs and culture that they would never understand one another, came together to fight as one. It was during the miners' strike, the longest strike in British history since 1926, when miners across the country went on strike in protest against coal mine closures. It became a bitter battle between the National Union of Miners and the prime minister,

Margaret Thatcher. During the strike Thatcher stopped all funds being sent to the miners and attempted to reduce the power of trade unions. The dispute brought hardship to families across the country, with their income stopped and donations struggling to get through. The media often painted the miners as 'the enemy', swaying public opinion along with Thatcher. They were the underdogs. A gay and lesbian group from London, watching this unfold, decided to mobilise. They knew what it was like to be demonised by both the establishment and the media. They fundraised and donated more money to the miners' cause than any other group in the UK. Because of the blocks Thatcher had put on donations to the National Union of Miners, people were encouraged to 'twin' with mining communities so that funds could be directly passed on. The London group was twinned with the Neath, Dulais and Swansea Valleys Miners' Support Group, so with their buckets of donations they headed to Wales in a minibus painted with the logo LGSM: Lesbians and Gays Support the Miners.

For the LGBT community this alliance was equally important. Miners' groups began to support, endorse and participate in various gay pride events throughout the UK, including leading London's Lesbian and Gay Pride parade in 1985. They came together to face common enemies and proved to be a powerful, united force, more than they could have imagined.

Mike Jackson, one of the original members, in an interview at Pride London said: 'It was about solidarity. Communities coming together and realising they have common purpose . . . We supported the miners unconditionally, because we knew that if trade union rights were taken away or diminished, everyone would suffer.'

Sometimes the most impactful partnerships are with allies you wouldn't expect, because they can provide networks, expertise and skills you might not have access to.

And getting together groups who are directly affected by or engaged with an issue but assumed to be on the 'opposite side' is a huge win. It instantly takes the teeth out of your opposition's argument. Think – who are the people everyone assumes are against your campaign? Then find them and start a conversation, convince them to come onto your side. Take inspiration from LGSM, and my dad.

There is strength in numbers and solidarity. And it is important in terms of strategy. If lots of campaigners, calling for similar change, are saying different things, perhaps even contradicting each other, the campaign will naturally be weakened. Work out your common cause.

Step Three: Create a Community

'Alone, we can do so little; together, we can do so much.'
— Helen Keller

One of the reasons I got into campaigning was the sense of community and belonging it created for me. In a 'selfie' world where individualism has become the norm, there's something magical about working as a group for a greater cause. At some level we all want to belong, and our values are a way of connecting us to like-minded people, knowing that we are understood.

The first time I went on a march, I came home vibrating from the energy and love I was surrounded by throughout the day. Complete strangers chanting together in unison, glancing in every direction and being met with warm smiles and laughter from fellow protestors. There was a feeling of kinship despite not knowing each other's names, because we all chose to be out there, on a Saturday morning, instead of lying in or having brunch with mates. We held similar values and felt connected by them. I think this particular protest was about climate change, but every march I've been on since gave me exactly the same feelings. Even the ones where we were viscerally angry, where a person's life was at risk. We may not have been smiling at each other during those protests, but our anger united us and we felt stronger as a collective – less hopeless, more positive.

Building a community for your campaign is as important for you as it is for your supporters.

No more Page 3

It was 2012 and the UK was in the middle of Olympics fever. The Summer Games were being hosted in London and we were winning gold medals. Lucy, like lots of Brits across the country, was swept up in the glory.

'During the Olympics I picked up a copy of the *Sun* to read on the train. The sun was shining and Britain was a place to be proud of. I noticed that there were no bare breasts on page 3, or on page 5. *Wow*, I thought, *they've dropped the boobs while the Olympics are on, possibly for editorial space, or perhaps as a mark of respect for all the different cultures visiting Britain.*

'I felt very pleased they'd done this as I carried on reading. But then I got to page 13 and there she was, a beautiful young woman in just her pants. And it made me feel incredibly sad. Hers was the largest image of any woman in this issue. Much larger even than those of Jessica Ennis who had just won a Team GB gold for her tremendous hard work.'

Lucy said that she'd grown up in a family where the *Sun* would be on the breakfast table, free for her to flick through as a child. She grew up feeling the same pressure and anxiety that a lot of young girls feel when they are surrounded by images of objectified women in the media. She compared herself to the topless models on page 3 and never felt good enough. Then she realised, as an adult, that she wasn't at fault. The *Sun* was.

She started her campaign, optimistically, by writing a letter to the editor. She got no reply, so she started a petition calling for 'No More Page 3'. Over 200,000 signatures quickly gathered; it seemed she wasn't the only one who didn't agree with the *Sun*'s sexualised images of women in a family newspaper.

It's important to note that Lucy did not see herself as a campaigner. That wasn't her world. At this point Lucy was an actress and novelist. She hadn't set out to become an activist. She simply had had enough and felt compelled to do something.

Lucy's campaign was all over the media and again she was optimistic that by the end of the year 'Page 3' would be scrapped. For months she kept her supporters engaged, did media interviews, ran social media channels, using every bit of her time and energy to keep up the noise around the campaign. She got to the end of the year and there was no sign of the *Sun* backing down. And Lucy was burnt out. As well as the work, she was drained by the misogyny she was getting online, the trolling by men telling her to shut up. She needed some time out.

In the new year she came back with a realisation: she couldn't do this alone. She needed support: not just people to help manage the social media and petition, both of which were growing but which also needed care and attention to keep people engaged, but she also needed emotional support. So that when there was a particularly horrible tweet, or when a depressing setback occurred, she had others who were in it with her, people to lean on. So she started letting go of control over the campaign brand and allowed young women across the UK the opportunity to start No More Page 3 groups in their area. Groups started springing up, from Brighton to Manchester; schools and universities declared support for the campaign, and campaign activity bubbled up across the country. It meant that Lucy no longer had to constantly come up with actions to maintain the campaign momentum; it was happening on its own and her role was simply to publicise it. Lucy speaks of this time as being a game-changer; not only did it give the campaign energy, but it felt bigger than before.

Yas Necati – No More Page 3 activist

Building up that community was helpful for Lucy, but the impact it had on her supporters was life-changing.

When Yas was fifteen a school art project at school led her to consider gender, what it meant to her and in society. The art project had steered the students to challenge themselves with conceptual questions. Yas realised that she had always pushed back at traditional 'female' or 'male' roles, that she was gender non-conforming, a feminist, but hadn't had the language before then to know that.

After putting energy into writing a blog to express the views she was formulating, she looked online, typing, 'What can I do to make change in wider society as a kid?' She found Change.org. 'Oh my god, I can sign petitions, that's what I can do. It became a gateway to activism. One day I got an email about the No More Page 3 campaign. Of course I signed it. But I wanted to do more.'

A protest was happening but it was during exam season and Yas was in the middle of her GCSEs. 'I probably would have gone but my parents would not have allowed it,' she tells me, and I believe that. Yas has an unstoppable drive once she has set her mind on something. She messaged the NMP3 team – asking if they would consider delaying the protest so GCSE students could go. They replied and suggested she organise her own, so that was exactly what she did!

After her exams, Yas organised a demonstration outside the *Sun*'s offices. It was a peaceful demo: they made origami flowers with messages written inside, and hung them up on the trees outside and on the building. Eight people came, including Yas's mum and sister. Yas remembers, 'I was buzzing from it – I felt like I was part of something bigger. I'm just a kid, going to school and these people have turned up because I asked them to. And the NMP3 team were supporting me. That intergenerational support, with older activists supporting the younger generation, felt special. Knowing that older people had faith in me as a young person gave me confidence and made me think – *I can do this.*'

After that Yas got a call from Lucy, inviting her to be part of the core NMP3 team.

'It changed who I am as a person – and how you feel about your place in the world and ability to make an impact. When you join a community, you have a really powerful collective voice. At the time it gave me so much strength and confidence, it was transformational.' It also formed lifelong friendships. 'We became good friends and some of them are my absolute best friends. Campaigning is often a deeply personal and emotional thing – we feel it to our core. To be alongside other people who feel that same issue to their core, is a bond like nothing else.

'I was young at the time, my ideas were only beginning to form and develop. And then I had this huge stepping

stone into feminism and activism. Getting involved with
the No More Page 3 campaign is one of the best things that
happened in my life. It was the beginning of moving from
campaigning as a personal interest to dedicating my life to
it. I'm now a professional campaigner in women's rights.

'After the campaign won, we went our separate ways,
into places we never would have if we hadn't had that
experience.'

The secrets to building a strong community

'The greatness of a community is most accurately measured by the compassionate actions of its members.'
— Coretta Scott King

You don't need hundreds of thousands of people to create change. And you don't all need to be in the same town or city either. You just need supporters who are genuinely engaged and get involved in the campaign. Creating a strong support base is an art; it takes time and thought. You want your supporters to feel as if they're really part of the fight. It's also the only way you'll win your campaign – no campaign was ever won by a single person, it takes a community of people.

There are lots of ways of building up a community, but essentially it's about your frame of mind. Think of your supporters as your campaign family, the people you want to share news with, turn to for advice, and every now and then let them know you're thinking of them. If you think in that way, your community-building will feel genuine and be much more successful. Here are some practical ways of building a community:

- **Collect contact details.** Being able to contact your supporters is one of the most important elements of both community-building and campaigning. Whether it's collecting email addresses to build an email list, starting a Facebook group or collecting numbers for a WhatsApp group, choose whatever feels easiest for you to manage and never miss a moment to tell people how they can join the group.

If you're collecting contact details, make sure people are explicitly opting into your communications (e.g. by ticking a box) in order to be compliant with GDPR. GDPR, or the General Data Protection Regulation, is a law that came into practice in 2016 and is about how to handle the data of anyone living in the EU in order to protect their privacy rights – including what they're explicitly opting into and how you're allowed to communicate with them. If you need more information, there are loads of resources available online to guide you with this.

• **Create a dialogue.** It's not really a community if there's no dialogue. Give your supporters opportunities to talk to each other, as well as talking to you. You do this by creating online and offline spaces for people to talk; by using Facebook Groups and posing questions, and by having meetups and getting to know each other. Always ask yourself: how can people engage with this online and how can they do more? The community will feel stronger, the more trust and contact there is within the group. Encourage your supporters to share information and news about the campaign within the group, give people permission to use the group to engage. They should start feeling like the campaign belongs to all of them.

- **Give your supporters a sense of purpose.** Since Lucy started the No More Page 3 campaign, people were asking her if there was anything they could do to help. Beyond a few campaign actions, she didn't really have more to give them. The idea of setting up NMP3 local groups meant that they could come up with their own campaign ideas and feel ownership over the campaign. When your campaign takes off, you'll inevitably have people asking how they can help. Give up some of the campaign power. Decentralising your campaign will give it more life, and create more activity, and that will help you win.
- **Crowdsourcing**. How can your supporters help win your campaign? When the snowball of supporters starts to gather more and more people, you'll realise that it's no longer just your family and friends but complete strangers backing you. This is when it starts to feel real! Crowdsource what you need for your campaign from your supporters. Ask if people

have any press expertise. If you need a photographer, maybe one of your supporters is a professional and wants to help. If you feel like you're running out of ideas on how to win the campaign, ask your supporters what the campaign could do next. Use this community for ideas and skills to help you with every step; it not only makes your community feel like they are needed and have a purpose, but is essential if you're campaigning on a shoestring.

- **Make their support highly visible.** Give people the opportunity to shout about their support. It creates a domino effect of more support, but also develops a sense of loyalty and affinity for the campaign in that person. I remember buying the No More Page 3 T-shirt before knowing much about the campaign, because they looked good and had a bigger message. Wearing that T-shirt was like telling the world, 'I'm a feminist.' It was bold and stood out. People wore them with pride, and in doing so, they were spreading the campaign message every-where they went. If your supporters are super-engaged, you don't really need that many of them. A campaign for Glastonbury to stop selling Native American headdresses won with just sixty-five people. Sixty-five active people backing your campaign is far more effective than 100,000 who only sign the petition and then do nothing. The petition starter, Daniel Round, got his signers to email the Glastonbury organisers and press office. Sixty-five people emailing the decision-maker and dominating their inbox made it feel like the issue was important. One day he got a call from the festival head office to tell him they would be banning the sale of headdresses at their next festival. When he won he said, 'Our petition, small in numbers but passionate in support, pushed this issue right up to Emily Eavis, and she listened.'

- **Communicate their work.** Every time a No More Page 3 group started, or an organisation came out in support of the campaign, Lucy made sure they shouted about it. In communicating the work of supporters, you are creating a loop which strengthens the feeling of community. Even people who are living far away start to feel like they're part of something bigger. How can people know what they can do to support if they haven't seen it done before? It's inspiring and models what you want others to do.

Step Four: Let's Get Tactical

'Great things are done by a series of small things brought together.'

— Vincent Van Gogh

I met Laura Coryton in 2014. She was a student who, during exam time when she was bored of revising, learned about the tax on sanitary products – the so-called 'tampon tax'. She learned that while certain things, like crocodile meat and Jaffa Cakes, were bizarrely exempt from VAT, tampons were taxed because they were deemed 'luxury items'. So she started a petition. Two years later Laura was on every news channel talking about how she overturned the tampon tax. How did she do it?

The tampon tax is an issue that feminists have been campaigning against for many years. Laura came along at a crucial moment in time – when the internet had made it easier than before to say something and have that something spread like wildfire. She managed to get thousands of people to sign her petition. And she was smart with what she did with those supporters. A typical campaign update from Laura read like an overexcited email from your best friend or sibling. Full of capital letters and exclamation marks. She would refer to the campaign as 'ours' and always had a question or request for her community of supporters: can anyone build a website for the campaign? Come to protest this Saturday, bring your banners! Write to your MP! She knew she would only win this mammoth of a battle (I mean, she was up against the Chancellor of the Exchequer!) with their help.

She had two main challenges when she started the campaign. Firstly, that despite this tax seeming ridiculous by anyone's standards, most people weren't aware of it. Secondly, the law itself was part of an EU regulation, meaning the ultimate decision-maker wasn't the UK government, but the European Parliament. So her strategy was to target the Chancellor, George Osborne, calling on him to negotiate a zero tax on sanitary products with the EU, and to get enough women (primarily) to know about this tax so that the Chancellor felt the pressure.

Her tactics were brilliant. She used a crocodile holding a tampon as her campaign image, setting the tone for the way she would approach this: with humour and irony. The campaign never took itself too seriously, it was never angry or worthy. It meant that when people found out, they laughed and wanted to share it with their friends. The image of the crocodile went viral. And this attitude was infectious; people across the country did ridiculous things with their tampons to make a point about the tax. After Taylor Swift released the song 'Bad Blood', a spoof was made by a group of comedians so that the song now called on Osborne to scrap the tax: 'Ladies, now we got bad blood. Our Super Pluses are adding up. Why you keep on taxing us?', with a hilarious video featuring superheroes Madame Ovary, Heavy Flow, Polly Sistic and Toksvig Shock. Girls posted pictures on Instagram of themselves doing ridiculous things with their tampons 'to get their money's worth', like wearing them as earrings. Somebody actually decorated their Christmas tree with tampons. This ripple effect went wide; famous comedians like Bridget Christie dedicated parts of their show to the tax. And while this was happening, Laura was sharing every bit of content created, followed by a request for them to write to their MPs to take this up in Parliament – where Osborne could be put on the spot. Cue Labour MP Paula Sherriff, who partnered up with Laura and took the issue on in Westminster. With Paula focusing on mobilising MPs and Laura on the public, they had their key audiences nailed. One key moment was a debate on the issue in the House of Commons, which was attended by far more female MPs than men. During the debate MP Stella Creasy famously wouldn't rest until the MP Bill Cash stopped referring to them as 'these products' and actually used the right language. She said she would not let him interject again 'unless he uses the term "sanitary towels and tampons" because I think it's really important in this House that we use the appropriate wording.' This made more headlines and more social media buzz. But it was a telling moment and a sign of just how great the period taboo was, that even in Parliament, in the heart of politics, it was not being spoken about openly.

During the 2015 general election, Laura saw her moment to clinch victory. With Labour and Liberal Democrats committing to scrapping the tax, this left the Conservatives as the prime target. During a televised debate David Cameron was confronted by a young person and asked his views about the tax. Put on the spot, he agreed to fighting it if he was elected. That's the beauty of campaigning during an election: you can secure wins when politicians are in their most vulnerable state and easily caught off guard. When the Conservatives won the election, they confirmed their commitment during the Autumn Budget speech. Osborne said that while the government would work with the EU to remove the tax, they would ring-fence money raised from the VAT and give it to women's rights organisations. Not only did the tampon tax campaign win (the UK government has committed to scrapping it by 2022), it has also created a fund for women in effect until the tax is gone, with money collected going toward causes like domestic violence.

How to be tactical

Tactics are the things you do to execute your strategy and Laura was brilliantly tactical. She kept focused on her strategy and had a good understanding of where she and her supporters could be effective, and where she needed other people to help.

Always ask supporters to do something

Create opportunities for potential supporters, influencers and even decision-makers to meet you, hear more about the issue, ask questions and hear what they can do to help. What was great about Laura's campaign was that it gave people different ways to be involved: those who wanted to write to their MP and engage politically could do that, and those who felt more comfortable using humour had the opportunity to do that too. And like Laura, even if the issue is serious, don't be afraid to be funny.

Know when you need help

There will be times when you get to this level and realise that you can't execute the tactic yourself – for example your tactic could be having a certain celebrity endorse the campaign. In Laura's case, she needed an advocate in Parliament to get MPs engaged and couldn't have done that without Paula Sherriff MP.

A tactical way of thinking

There are always more tactics out there; every new technology and different target presents new strategic and tactical opportunities. So while it is important to learn some things that have worked for other campaigns, it is more important to learn this pattern of thinking so that you can identify the right thing to do in new situations and creatively dream up what should be done.

Pivot if you need to

There may be times when you've been campaigning for a long time and the decision-maker just isn't budging. These are the moments when it's smart to put that to one side and pivot your campaign to another target. When Lucy was running the No More Page 3 campaign and was getting nothing from the *Sun*, she changed her strategy and targeted the companies who were advertising in the paper. If she could pressurise them to stop advertising in the *Sun* then she could hit them where it hurt: their income. Lego was one of these companies, so they pivoted and a new petition was started, calling for the brand to stop advertising their children's products in the *Sun*. It worked: after two years of advertising, Lego ended its partnership with the *Sun*. Though the company said that their contract with the newspaper came to a natural end, it was telling that they never renewed. This was the first big victory for the campaign. Pivoting doesn't mean you stop targeting your primary decision-maker, you will always return to them!

Dictionary of tactics

The following list is not exhaustive but is a useful starting point to understand the scope of things you can do and when to apply the different tactics.

Petitions

If you need to show or prove that there is strength of feeling behind your campaign, a petition is the way to do it. Petitions are one of the oldest campaign tools that exist but with the growth of the internet, online petitions have made it unbelievably easy to gather signatures. Rather than spending a rainy Saturday on your local high street or traipsing around a university campus to collect names, you can share an online petition on email, in online forums, Facebook groups or WhatsApp groups, and tweet your link to journalists and celebrities. And petitions are particularly useful when something is causing outrage on social media. When the facts about the tampon tax started to spread, instead of, or as well as, venting on Facebook and using the hashtag on Twitter, people could sign a petition. It's like casting a net into the ocean and catching fish; rather than these hashtags and outraged tweets going into the abyss, someone is collecting them so that the strength of support is clearly evident – a useful tactic in putting pressure on the decision-maker, and not allowing them to brush the issue off as concerning only a handful of people.

Demonstrations

A demonstration is a mass meeting of your supporters, a physical protest. They usually start with a march and end at a meeting point where campaigners make speeches. They are a good way of building a sense of community and solidarity in the campaign, and can be a good tactic to make the decision-maker see the support you have and know you are serious. And you don't have to be a seasoned activist to do this; Laura told me that the first demonstration she ever went on was the one she organised herself. It's intimidating to hold your first demonstration but do it and you'll realise it's a lot easier than you imagined. And be prepared, because like anything with your campaign, it won't always go completely to plan. When Laura organised her first demonstration, it was to deliver her petition to 10 Downing Street. Around thirty people turned up; they had T-shirts and banners and the national media covered it. Another time she organised a protest and just one or two people turned up. It was disappointing but Laura realised it wasn't a reflection of the support in her campaign. Sometimes it doesn't work out the way you planned – learn from the experience and keep going.

Polls

Opinion polls, or surveys, can provide you with a news story as well as another statistic to add to the case you're building in your bid to win. New stats are particularly useful if there hasn't been much research or discussion about your issue before you started to campaign. Before you start, think in headlines to figure out what you want your poll to say, to provide you with a fresh angle to the campaign. For example, Laura could have conducted a survey ahead of the General Election to ask people if they would be more likely to vote for someone if they backed the tampon tax campaign, helping her to persuade the Conservative Party to back it. But you need to make sure you craft your questions carefully so that they're not biased, and be prepared to get results you're not expecting – that's the beauty of asking people, sometimes they surprise you. Look around online; there are some great free tools out there to poll or survey people, but before you do this make sure you have a good dissemination strategy. Your survey won't be very useful if only twenty people fill it out (unless those twenty people are highly influential to your campaign). There are professional polling companies out there whom you can pay to run the poll for you, from crafting the questions to asking the public, but they usually cost a lot so this is only worth doing it if it's a crucial question to winning the campaign and you can get access to some funding.

Lobby local MPs

Asking supporters to write to their MP to support your campaign is a strong tactic because politicians are more likely to listen to people in their constituency. If your campaign involves a vote of some kind in Parliament, you'll need to contact as many MPs as possible so that they vote the way you need. So if you have supporters across the country, it's a great way of getting your message to lots of MPs at once.

If you use this tactic, encourage supporters to write the message in their own words, including any personal experience they have of the issue. Personal and tailored emails are more likely to grab an MP's attention than a standard email that's been copied and pasted. There's more information about how to lobby MPs, including how to find contact details, in the chapter about decision-makers.

Campaign events

Like a demonstration, a campaign event is a great way for supporters to come together, meet each other and meet you. Campaign events can be anything from hosting an expert speaker for a question-and-answer session, a panel event featuring experts and influential people in your campaign, or presenting some news or fresh research, like the results of a survey. You could even do a campaign event to launch your campaign, if you have already established a network of people to engage. It can be a little stressful to organise something like this, so make sure you have people who can help you and leave yourself enough time to plan. Here's an outline of a very basic event plan to get you started:

EVENT TITLE: Campaign launch

PROJECT LEAD

	Week 1	Week 2	Week 3	Week 4	Week 5	Event week	Week after
Event name and description	■						
Venue options found	■						
Venue booked	■						
Speakers approached	■						
First speaker confirmed		■					
Invite guests			■				
Start to push event on social			■				
Confirm all speakers				■			
Contact press					■		
Practice streaming event on social					■		
Event reminder to all guests and speakers						■	
Email guests with follow up action							■

Creative stunts

The Bad Blood spoof was successful because it was silly, ripping off a well-known hit, and it was shareable. Your stunts are more likely to get shared on social media and in the press if they are unusual, creative or silly. In Switzerland, the campaign to end the tampon tax turned thirteen fountains blood red in the capital city – the campaigners were not only making a statement about the tax, they were challenging the taboo around menstruation by making people confront it in a public space. Think about the message you want to convey and then spend an hour brainstorming ideas, with no limits, and see what you come up with. Make sure a stunt doesn't distract from your campaign – you don't want to do something so controversial that it becomes the subject of discussion rather than the issue at hand. And make it visual, with a good photographer to take the picture. The primary aim is to get media coverage and journalists need a good-quality image if they're going to cover a stunt.

Open letters

Open letters are letters to your decision-maker that are published in a newspaper to create public pressure and stir up debate. They need to be newsworthy so that the newspaper will publish it, so try to include something new in the letter. One way of doing this is to find high-profile and influential people to co-sign your letter. When I worked on the campaign for compulsory sex and relationships education, *The Times* published a joint letter from the UK Youth Parliament and 500 other organisations, MPs and celebrities. It was a newsworthy letter because it was signed by so many high-profile people, including politicians from all parties and celebs like Davina McCall who had spoken out about sex education in the past. My colleague Fiona and I hit the phones over a two-week period and asked each person directly. It was a slog but worth it for what we got in return – a *Times* front page which catapulted the campaign onto the Parliamentary agenda.

Adverts

An open letter can also be placed as an advert in a newspaper. You need funds for this, but if you can get a big enough space in the right newspaper, it can be very effective. Make sure to think about which newspapers your decision-maker is more likely to read or be influenced by. You can also use adverts to send a message to the public, and it doesn't have to be in a newspaper. Most public spaces have advertising windows and boards; find out who runs them and get quotes for hiring the space.

Cue the four dads, three Remainers and a Leaver, who were frustrated at the hypocrisy of politicians during the Brexit debate. After a pub conversation ranting about politics, and about how badly certain politicians came across when you saw their previous tweets, they schemed to turn these tweets into posters for billboards. Initially they did it without permission: the first poster was pasted in the middle of the night by the men dressed in high-vis. It featured a tweet by David Cameron that read 'Britain faces a simple and inescapable choice – stability and strong government with me or chaos with Ed Miliband.' After that the group – which named itself Led by Donkeys, in reference to a First World War phrase, 'lions led by donkeys', about the infantry and the generals that led them – started a crowdfunder so that they could pull off their stunts legally. To their utter surprise, they raised over £300,000 and are the largest crowd-funded political campaign in the UK.

Hijack their hashtag

Social media has opened up the world of tactics to another level. While companies and politicians have a certain amount of power when it comes to traditional media, social media is one space where they are playing catch-up. You can take advantage of that to amusing results. When Lucy was campaigning for Tesco to stop selling caged eggs, she thought Easter would be a good time for a campaign action (because, eggs!). So during the Easter weekend, whenever Tesco posted anything about Easter eggs, she messaged her supporters and they bombarded those very posts with questions about their caged eggs. Hundreds of supporters kept this up all weekend, leaving whoever was on social media duty at Tesco HQ over the holiday in a fluster, copying and pasting the same company statement over and over. This did them no favours; it came across as corporate and lacking a human touch, as if they weren't really listening and addressing people's concerns. This was shortly before Tesco asked Lucy for a meeting, and no doubt that tactic had something to do with it. So keep an eye on your decision-maker's social media output, and if you can use their hashtags or campaigns to your advantage, it's a great way of getting their attention.

Media 101

'There is only one thing worse than being talked about, and that's not being talked about.'

— Oscar Wilde

Getting your campaign in the news is vital in communicating your message and influencing decision-makers. Before you start, make sure you understand how the media work and what journalists are looking for.

Traditional vs new media

We have grown up with broadcast news and newspapers as being the trusted source of news, and this still holds to some degree. These are trusted and consumed by influential people. But in today's twenty-four-hour news cycle with information spreading faster than ever on the internet, how do you decide what to focus on?

When we talk about traditional media, we're talking about:

- Print newspapers and magazines
- Online news channels like BuzzFeed and Huffington Post

- Broadcast – TV and radio programmes
- Podcasts – those that have large audiences

New media, or social media, are platforms where we create our own content, like Twitter, Facebook, Instagram and YouTube. We can even start our own podcasts now. Previously, the only way to get your message out to masses was through the gatekeepers at the traditional channels – journalists, editors, the news desk, the features desk, the letters page . . . but since the rise of social media platforms, we are able to cut out the middle-man and speak directly to audiences. Campaigners have taken advantage of this: they've realised they don't need to wait for the news sites to decide if their story is worth telling because if their social media audience likes their content, it will get shared and distributed just as far, and sometimes further.

Like most things in life, the answer is about balance. Use both, for different purposes. If you want to get your message taken seriously by influential people, traditional media is a great validator. It can give you the kudos you need for people to trust your message. If you want to reach a lot of people, and you want to do it fast, social media is better.

Media dos and don'ts

Make sure it's news

Don't assume that just because you're interested in the issue, that others will be too. You need to *make* them interested. Ask yourself – what's new about what I'm saying? Create the news hook if you need to. Things that tend to pique a journalist's interest are if you are saying something unexpected, there is a powerful, personal story, something is being announced, there are new statistics or research, something is linked to an important or signifi-cant date, or there is someone high-profile involved. If you don't have any of these, then create one of them!

Build a press list

Don't send your press release to any old journalist. Start off by researching people who have written about the issue in the past, and start compiling names and contact details. When you know whom you're pitching to, be strategic by going through the journalist's previous work and mention that in your pitch. Giving your pitch a personal touch will make you stand out and more likely to engage the journalist.

Pick up the phone

Use your phone, it's a dying tradition but so effective. Once you know who you're pitching to and have sent the email, follow up with a phone call. Don't be intimidated but make sure you get straight to the point; journalists are busy people. You're just giving them a nudge and another opportunity to hear about your story. Have all the information out in front of you – the figures and the story – and ask if they need any more information from you. Be friendly and polite and thank them for their time.

Build lasting relationships

If you get a journalist's attention, keep in touch with them and cultivate that relationship. This is one of the best relationships you can develop when campaigning, because if you find a journalist that cares about your issue, they will want to follow your campaign and continue to write about it. And some of the best journalists see themselves as activists; they use news to draw attention to a problem and continue to cover the issue until something changes. They can become your best advocate, providing you with a megaphone each time you say something.

Be reactive

Follow the news cycle, create Google Alerts to let you know when something relevant to your campaign comes up, and follow relevant journalists on social media so that you're ready to respond if something happens with your campaign, or the issue it relates to. Good campaigning is about being flexible and fast – just because your strategy said you should do X, Y and Z, if something big happens in the news, capitalise on that moment to draw attention to your campaign and change your plans. You can't predict the news, so always be ready to drop what you're doing and respond to external events.

Give them visuals

When you're planning your stunts, think in images. Journalists want content. Anything you can add that's interesting and visual could increase the likelihood of your story getting out there. With social media dominating the way we consume news, and particularly video, any footage with your story is also helpful. Try to get as good quality material as possible, and if it's a stunt, send the images as soon as it happens.

It's a win–win

Remember that it's a journalist's job to look for stories. People sometimes feel bad about pestering journalists, and if you approach them with that mindset, you won't get far. You want to get the issue covered, and they are looking for stories. As long as you're friendly and polite, you should feel good about reaching out; you're helping them do their job.

It's a tactic, not the victory

Don't get caught up in getting media coverage for the sake of it. Be strategic and plan out the moments when you want to get publicity, it will keep the quality of news that you give to journalists at a higher standard and will stop you from wasting your time. Getting news coverage of your campaign is another way of spreading your message and sometimes it puts added pressure on the decision-maker. But it shouldn't be thought of as the end goal. Your campaign is trying to change the decision-maker's mind, not the journalist's.

Let the story go

Once you've pitched and been interviewed, you can't do anything to control what the journalist writes. This might mean that they take an angle you weren't expecting, and maybe that doesn't tell a positive story about your campaign. That's OK – it can feel like the end of the world at the time but by the next day, no one will remember. Learn from the experience and move on.

Lights! Camera! Action!
Preparing for interviews

'I get nervous when I don't get nervous. If I'm nervous
I know I'm going to have a good show.'

— Beyoncé

Media interviews can be nerve-wracking, but with prep-
aration you can smash them. There was a famous interview of Jeremy Corbyn during the General Election in
2017 when he appeared on Radio 4's *Woman's Hour* for
an interview with Emma Barnett.

Corbyn was asked about Labour's election pledge that
promised free childcare for 1.3 million children in the
UK. When asked how much the policy would cost, a
question he might have expected, things started to go
wrong.

Corbyn: It will cost – it will obviously cost a lot to do
so, we accept that.
Barnett: I presume you have the figures.
Corbyn: Yes I do . . . It does cost a lot to do, the point
I'm trying to make is, making it universal so that we
are in a position to make sure that every child gets it.
Barnett: So how much?
Long silence.

Barnett: You don't know it? You're logging into your iPad here, you've announced a major policy and you don't know how much it will cost?

It was the stuff of nightmares, and a lesson in preparing for a media interview. For Corbyn's team, it would have been quite easy to predict this particular question, which was mistake number one. His attempt to pivot to another point was painfully obvious. And despite reaching for his iPad right in front of the interviewer, he continued to insist he knew the answer. I have huge empathy for anyone who has to endure such a car crash, and quite honestly you are never likely to be put under the same level of pressure as a prospective prime minister; it's the job of the media to put a politician through rigorous, difficult questions. But the lessons above are important nonetheless. The key thing for you to remember is that it will get easier and better with practice. When I first started I hated the entire experience, I would feel physically sick and couldn't eat a thing for the entire day until it was over. But as they got more frequent, I put less importance on them, and actually started to have fun, believe it or not. You see, your media interview will be only one of many important moments in your campaign. So don't let it overwhelm you, prepare the hell out of it, and then enjoy it.

Three key messages

You are passionate about the campaign and so excited to be interviewed that you want to tell the interviewer everything there is to know about your campaign. Don't do that. Too much information is hard for a listener to digest and also hard for you to remember. Boil the campaign down to three key messages: what's the problem, why you care and what people can do to help. Write down your key messages and work on them until they feel compelling and urgent. You want people to come away and understand why the problem is critical, and know how they can help to solve it.

When in doubt, bridge

Every person that's ever been interviewed knows that no matter how much you prepare, you will at times get asked questions you aren't expecting and don't know the answer to, or don't want to answer. When this happens, use these 'bridging' phrases to get you back to your key messages:

'What's really important here is . . .'
'The key issue . . .'
'Let's keep in mind . . .'
You may have other phrases that work better for you;

the point is to move away from the interviewer's question and back to your key messages. Once you start doing this, you'll see common bridging when you listen to interviews and you'll wonder how you've never noticed it before. And remember that nobody wants you to fail so if the question throws you off, bridge. The interviewer won't really mind; unless you're a politician or CEO that they're desperate to interrogate about the story of the day, they generally want the best out of you, so it makes a great interview.

Practise, practise, practise! And then forget it

The first time I ever did a media interview, I was caught off guard: I was asked to say a few words on the spot about a campaign I was supporting, when I happened to be in a BBC radio studio. I never listened back to it and dread to think what came out of my mouth. I wasn't prepared and felt a little ambushed. The best advice I can give you about being interviewed is to prepare; practise what you're going to say to a friend or colleague. Record yourself on a phone, or ask someone to record you, so you can watch it back and get a good idea of what you sound and look like. Practise it a few times, and then leave the notes to one side. There is too much emphasis put on seeming polished and slick – I don't know about you but when I listen to and watch interviews, I'm much more drawn to the people who seem 'real'. They're not overly slick and shiny, they pause, maybe they stumble over a few words, and this makes them seem human and easy to connect to. As a campaigner you're trying to persuade people, you're not being judged on the same level as politicians, so don't feel like you need to sound like one. And certainly don't aim for it; your power is in your authenticity.

WTF is social media?

First of all – let's get the elephants out of the room. Social media can be intimidating because we think it's dominated by a certain type of millennial that is always online and has a million followers. And then there are the horror stories about trolls and online abuse.

I'll be honest, some of these worries are valid and I have some tips on how to navigate them. But I also think they can be exaggerated in the media, and that sadly puts people off from using social media to have their voice heard. So don't avoid it, just use this guide to help you get around.

Five tips to becoming a social media activist

1. **Pick your channel wisely.** There are so many platforms out there that you could use: if you're an old hand at social media then you might be across them all, but if you're new to this then I would pick one or two for your campaign. Twitter is great for connecting with influential people like journalists, MPs and campaigning organisations. Facebook groups are great for building a dialogue with your own supporters. And Instagram is growing in use with the public, so it's a good place for spreading your message if you're good with visuals.

2. **Schedule content.** Unless you have a lot of time to spare, or are a social media junkie, you will never be able to keep up with the pace of interactions and constant news. Use my 70/30 rule for the content you're posting – 70% of content should be pre-planned and scheduled to post at specific times and 30% should be reactive. Spend a few hours a week deciding what you want to be talking about to your supporters each day, draft a few posts that you can then schedule on a social media management platform like Hootsuite that lets you schedule content across platforms. If something is happening with your campaign issue, then be reactive, respond to the news. This will help you get established as a relevant voice on the topic.

3. **Build a distribution list.** If you're preparing content for social media, you can't just post it online on your profile and expect it to go viral or even do that well (unless you already have a large following). Just like building a press list, build a distribution list of all the groups, influencers and pages that would be interested in your content. Create tailored posts targeted at those specific audiences and give them a chance to engage, by asking a question or urging them to share.

4. **Pay attention to the numbers.** To get good at

social media, you need to pay attention to the engagement data and learn. First of all, do some research and find out the best days and times to post. This is always changing, because our behaviour as a society is constantly changing as the ways we work, socialise and have access to the internet evolve, so the best thing is to do some research online. Once you know when to post, test content and pay attention to how much engagement you're getting. Keep testing and recording what you learn – why does one post get more engagement over another? Is there something about the images or the language you're using that your supporters particularly engage with? Keep testing, learning and adapting to build a strong social media profile.

5. **Stay safe from abuse.** It's a sad truth that sometimes speaking up can result in online abuse. This is particularly true for marginal groups, i.e. women, or people of colour. Thankfully, social media platforms are starting to take this more seriously, but the reality is far from perfect. Firstly, if you are receiving abuse, report it using the tools on the platform you're using. If it continues, report it to the police. Online abuse is now regarded as a crime and should be taken seriously. In terms of your campaigning, it's OK to either step away from social media for a

bit, if it's getting too much, or to ignore the trolls and continue. Everyone responds and reacts differently; do what's right for you at the time. And above all, get support, because you're not alone. Go to stoponlineabuse.org.uk/resources for a list of groups that offer help if you're dealing with abuse. Read more on this topic in the chapter, 'Self-Care for Activists' (p. 170).

Magid Magid

Magid Magid is a former refugee who became the Lord Mayor of Sheffield in 2018. From tweeting that 'Donald Trump is a wasteman' to playing the 'Imperial March' from *Star Wars* and the *Superman* theme at his inauguration ceremony, he has used his job as a way of making politics more accessible to young people, and drawing attention to racism and 'post-Brexit xenophobia'. His appointment attracted national media attention, as he is the first Somali, the youngest person ever, and the first Green Party councillor, to hold the role in Sheffield. After his term as Mayor, in the 2019 European elections Magid was elected as an MEP for Yorkshire and Humberside.

Magid caught my eye when, in his inaugural portrait, he squatted on the Council chamber banister wearing green Dr. Martens boots; the image then went viral on Twitter. Most would have been expecting the Lord Mayor of Sheffield to be another old white guy, maybe sat in the Council chamber on a throne. Magid turned that image on its head and, like me, the internet loved it. Speaking to BuzzFeed he said, 'I guess it's not your average photo for a Lord Mayor but I thought it represented me well enough. Firstly, it was a massive health and safety hazard as it was a big drop. But I was first standing on it as I thought it would make an interesting shot.' It's inspiring to see someone who had so many odds against him, being so young, being a refugee, being part of a small party, make it as Mayor and become such an icon for everyday activism. He said he knew nothing of politics when he started to get into it, and taught himself watching YouTube videos. 'I thought about that phrase – do politics or politics will do you – and so I thought, f*ck it, I'll get involved.'

His inaugural Mayor portrait, squatting in Dr. Martens on expensive council furniture, has become typical of Magid's approach to politics: he breaks the rules, defies expectations and uses social media to get his message out there. And inevitably he goes viral. When I asked him why he picked social media as his main channel he said, 'Who on earth reads the council's website?!' Good point.

If it sounds like I'm gushing, well I am. Magid has broken so many rules while inspiring a whole generation of people to engage in politics. And he's done it in the most honest and genuine way. So when I spoke to him, I made him tell me his secret recipe, so that I could tell all of you. Here are Magid's top tips to becoming a social media activist:

Magid Magid's social media top tips:

1. People's attention spans are getting so short – there's so much info out there, you've got to cut through all of that. I do it by being super-creative, and then weaving my political message in after.

2. Be blunt, straightforward, and don't try and feel like you have to win everyone over. I've learned that it's more powerful to be unapologetically yourself in every aspect. People want to see themselves in you and relate to you – and they will only relate if you are honest about who you are and what you believe in.

3. Be different and take risks – look at what other people are doing and think about the value you can add that is different. Then people will listen because you're doing or saying something new.

4. There's no secret formula, because then everyone would use it! I don't always know what I'm gonna do, I'm learning as I'm going. So don't be hard on

yourself, give yourself a break – all you can do is keep learning. You should be thinking, 'This is a bit weird but let's give,' don't hold yourself back from fear of getting it wrong.

5. Your energy is limited, so ignore the trolls. It's easy to rage out online when someone says something personal to you, but no one in the history of the internet has ever won an argument online. You'll never see me debating like that with people, and I get a lot of people trying to start arguments with me. It doesn't mean you shouldn't point out BS, call it out when you see it, but negative campaigning doesn't work. Positivity breeds positivity.

Step Five: Winning (or, How to Keep Going)

'If you're an activist, you've already won.'

— Me

You may never know when you're going to win, so you need to be prepared. Luke and Brian's campaign to stop Brian's deportation was won in a matter of weeks. Lucy thought when she started No More Page 3 that she would be done in a matter of months. Two years later they were able to claim victory and Lucy learned a lot about sustaining herself during a campaign. And Richard Ratcliffe hasn't seen his wife Nazanin in person for over three years now; all the while, he's been fighting for her to be released from an Iranian prison.

Imagine a loved one goes abroad for a holiday. They get arrested, with no idea why. And they have no right to consular support that could help prove their innocence. When Nazanin left for a holiday in April 2016 with her one-year-old daughter Gabriella, she couldn't have imagined that she would be forced into solitary confinement at one of Iran's most notorious prisons. Or that for 1,163 days (and counting), Gabriella would be separated from her mother and father, and forget how to speak English.

And her husband, Richard, could never have imagined that after his wife left with their little girl, he would go on to spend his every waking hour retelling his wife's story. Every sleepless night wondering if she had eaten that day. Every morning devastated that this wasn't all a horrible dream.

It's not commonly known that your protection as a British citizen when overseas is up to the discretion of the UK government. Like most of us, Richard and Nazanin had always thought they could rely on their country to advocate for them if they were ever in danger abroad. This just isn't the case. Before speaking out, Richard spent a month after Nazanin's arrest trying to get the UK government to help behind closed doors. He expected what you or I might in this situation, that the government would do everything in their power to get their citizen back to safety.

They were both students when they met; Richard, working on his PhD, had attended a conference and been introduced to Nazanin through a friend of a friend. They later met for coffee a week later in London, at the National

Theatre. When he speaks about their first date, his face warms. He said they just clicked. 'It's almost like coming home, we had one of those conversations that was so easy. By date two, Nazanin was very much like, are you serious or not?' By date three she had told her mum about Richard. That was in 2007, when Richard was in his early thirties. By 2009 they were married. They had no idea that six years later they'd be catapulted into a life-changing situation that would cause them and their baby girl the kind of trauma that no one is prepared for.

I asked Richard about that last moment when they saw each other in 2016; does he replay it over in his mind?

'It was at Gatwick airport. We'd had lunch and Gabriella was running up and down the entire length of the departure lounge, running into all these poor people with their suitcases, giggling away.'

They were going for Norooz, Iranian New Year. That was 17th March 2016; they were supposed to be back on 3rd April.

'I have a clear memory of it and I've been asked about that moment a lot. But I don't lament the last moment, it could have been more romantic, but I try to hold on to the normal things. There's a way you can Hollywood-ise everything and I try not to do that. Nazanin does dwell on these moments in prison, and it's hard for her, it's bittersweet.'

When Nazanin got arrested on landing in Iran, the advice he had been given was, 'Leave it to the experts and she has a better chance of being released.' But weeks later, having followed this advice, he saw little indication that anything was happening. He had read about how Iman Ghavami started a petition for his British–Iranian sister Ghoncheh who was placed in solitary confinement for attending a men's volleyball match. After six months of campaigning and 775,000 signatures, the public pressure helped get her released. So a month after Nazanin was arrested, Richard went public and started a petition.

From struggling to be heard by the government, he found people who wanted to listen. When they signed in their thousands, Richard could go back to his wife and say: 'We're not alone.' Richard says that when Nazanin is out, he wants to show her all the comments that have been left on the petition, the messages of support, solidarity and hope. This is what has kept them both going during the worst months of their lives. In one of his updates, Richard wrote to signers: 'Your witness, your care is what gives power to my pen. It is what gives us hope. My friends can testify how poor I am at responding to messages. But my family and I read your comments closely, are kept stronger by them.' And the campaigning seemed to be working. They finally met with the Foreign

Office the day before Richard was delivering the petition to Number 10 Downing Street. It shouldn't have taken this long, but the cogs were starting to turn.

The 1,166,478 people who have signed have given Richard and Nazanin a voice when they've felt voiceless. The petition levelled out the playing field. As the signatories grew, Richard's voice became more and more prominent in the media. When the issue was debated in Parliament, Richard urged his signers to write to their MPs. His MP, Tulip Siddiq, who has tirelessly fought her constituents' battle since day one, has used the petition as evidence of public interest in the case to raise questions in the Commons. As our representatives, MPs need our voices to strengthen their argument when they're debating on the bench. This family, who might not otherwise have had the power and privilege to influence, have had the Foreign Secretary and Prime Minister address them directly.

Every added signature gives Richard the strength to keep going. Though he has been close to powerful people, he still feels very much in the dark; Nazanin's freedom has been so close at times he could almost touch it. Yet she is still there today, hundreds of miles away from home.

How to keep going

An important tip for any campaign is to prepare to keep going. You should never go in thinking you are going to win quickly, and knowing this will make it easier for you to accept defeat when things inevitably don't go your way. Prepare for the long game, it will keep you focused, strong and difficult to ignore.

Being present and focused

I asked Richard whether he had ever imagined it was going to take this long, and how on earth he has kept going for so long. 'When it first happened, at the time I remember even thinking, it would be better if she stayed in for the weekend so I can go and get her next weekend. And then, I hope she's back in time to eat the food because I'd done a big shop.' Richard has an ability to be both present and think very far ahead. It stops him from going mad, I suppose, because he's both able to focus on what is needed from him this very second, and also to keep going to eventually be reunited with Nazanin. It keeps him patient. He had been prepared by others at first that she could be imprisoned for three to six months. At the beginning he didn't think beyond nine months. Three years later he has the calm and focus of someone who knows he must keep sane for the family; he says he is in 'battle mode'.

Prioritise and delegate

You can't do everything. When your campaign starts to overwhelm, you need to start prioritising tasks and delegating. 'I feel like I juggle badly. Always dropping balls and beating myself up for not doing things. Work has been under strain since this all happened but they've been incredibly understanding. On a day like yesterday [when the UK government announced that Nazanin would be given diplomatic protection, meaning that the UK no longer regarded her case as simply a consular matter and had raised it to the level of a legal dispute between Britain and Iran], I didn't go into work and no questions were asked. They accept that they are paying me for a full-time job and I'm not working full-time hours.'

Richard has to make multiple decisions on a regular basis, about what to say, who to give an interview to, what to ask his supporters to do. It can get too much and so leaning on those around you is vital.

We generally find it hard to ask for help because we've been taught that asking for help is a weakness. We convince ourselves that we should be able to do it all by ourselves, as if that's what everyone else does. But it's not true, we all need support and some are better at asking and taking it than others. Think about the times you have offered to help someone and whether that person really took you up on the offer. Too often we talk about support but never actually give and receive it.

It can be hard to ask when you're not used to it. I know, I have to push myself every time. And even now I can feel so overwhelmed inside but appear calm and collected, and nobody would know I needed support. But here are some truths (that I have to remind myself of): asking for help is a sign of strength, it shows you know what you need and are confident in asking for it. Helping each other creates stronger bonds, and brings us closer to those around us. Getting support will make your work better. And people want to help you so when they offer, take it. And when you need it, ask for it.

Here's a guide designed to make asking for help easier:

1. Write down a list of all the tasks that need to be done.
2. Prioritise the tasks in order of urgency, in colour blocks. Red – it needs to be done ASAP. Orange – needs to be done soon-ish. Green – this can wait for now.
3. Forget the green for now. This is what is called

deprioritising – you cannot do everything and some tasks simply need to be left behind. The trick is to do this in a conscious way, rather than accidentally letting things slip and making you feel disorganised and out of control. And don't worry, you won't lose anything by leaving these tasks behind for now; you still have them written down and can come back to them in the future if they are important.

4. Put a name down next to each red and orange task of someone who can help you complete it. There may be certain tasks that can only be done by you, which is fine, but the idea is to lighten your overall load.

5. Ask the people you've listed for help – and be specific about what you need and when you need it by.

Learning from failure

Failure is inevitable and it's important you don't dwell on mistakes. Richard talks about being in 'battle mode' in the sense that he doesn't have the time or head space to look back, he has to keep moving forwards as a matter of survival. 'I realise that people may think some of my actions in the past were a mistake. When I've put a strain on our family because of decisions I've made.

When the Iranian authorities tried to pressure Nazanin into becoming a spy for them, she told me but didn't want me to reveal it. But when she went on hunger strike, which I didn't want her to do, I felt compelled to reveal the pressures they were putting on her. I felt I had to, I refuse for them to play games with us. It's an open question whether that was a mistake and if I should have kept on the good side of the Iranian authorities.'

Richard's campaign is high stakes; at times it feels like a truly life-or-death situation – Nazanin has gone through several spells of feeling suicidal. There are also other Iranian prisoners whose families are campaigning for their release. So every action he takes feels like it can fall like a domino, with consequences he sometimes can't foresee and that may impact so many others. How do you campaign when there is so much at risk? So many opportunities to get it wrong?

One of the ways is by reminding yourself that even your mistakes are worthwhile. In her book *How to Fail*, Elizabeth Day explores the lessons that failure teaches us. When Day interviewed the author James Frey he talked about how every book he had written and thrown away before his bestseller, *A Million Little Pieces*, was not a failure but necessary. 'I just look at them as part of the process.' But this isn't something that comes easily to us, embracing failure or even thinking of setbacks as process rather than failure. Day says this is because 'we live in an age of curated perfection', with social media as an alternative reality where we exist as our best, more successful, popular self. Opinions on Twitter are battled out, the drive to be 'right' overrides any regard for truth. But this is all limiting, and as you journey through your campaign, for both the health of the campaign, and your own mind, go into it embracing failure and expecting to get things wrong.

In Silicon Valley, there is a mantra: 'Fail fast, fail often.' The philosophy is to take risks, try a lot of things, do it fast, learn quickly what worked, iterate your idea, and repeat. The idea is that, the faster you fail, the quicker you will get to your goal.

You will face setbacks in your campaign; don't dwell on them, just be thankful for the opportunity to learn from them because they will get you to victory quicker. Take this approach in every moment that doesn't go as planned; if a meeting with an influential person for your campaign doesn't end as you'd expected, take a moment and reflect on why. What can you learn from that and will you approach your campaign differently as a result? If a campaign video that you made doesn't get as much engagement as you had expected, don't just create another video in the same way. Ask yourself why, ask your supporters for their views. Be open to learning, always. It is liberating and will make you a stronger, happier campaigner.

Ramp up, slow it down

There will be times when you are inundated and need help from those around you to manage, and other times when things go quiet and that can feel nerve-wracking. Has the moment passed? Will I ever get that kind of exposure again? Does anyone still care? First off, don't panic. Every campaign goes through peaks and troughs; it's the nature of media that an issue will come and go from the news, you just need to make sure you're ready to ride the wave when it happens.

Secondly, realise that you don't need to and can't do everything all the time. So there will be times when media is more important, and other times that it's a better use of your time and energy to focus on getting political support behind the scenes. For Richard, it was essential in that first year of speaking out about Nazanin being imprisoned and calling for the government's support that he capitalised on media and public attention. It was about building up the campaign's awareness, getting Nazanin's story out there and keeping people engaged to stay with him in the fight. Three years on and it is less important to secure publicity all the time; most people across the country know the campaign or are familiar with his wife's name. Now it's more important that he is keeping up attention and pressure with the government and allies who can help with the 'backstage stuff' as he calls it. The media and public engagement has taken a back seat, and he will step forward at times when it's particularly needed, such as when Nazanin has gone on hunger strike and he needs to draw attention to that.

Know when you need to ramp up the noise, and what to do when it slows down. Don't panic about the quiet times, enjoy them, use them to focus in other areas.

Being flexible

By now you have a strong strategy that is meticulously planned. Do not stick to it. What I mean by this is, follow it but don't be so rigid that you can't veer away or even make serious turns in another direction. The point in your strategy is that it is a plan – you know which direction you're going in because you have worked hard to understand the situation and decide what is best. But things will happen in the external environment that you will not have planned for and so your planned tactics might not still be relevant.

When Boris Johnson, the former Foreign Secretary,

spoke about Nazanin's case in Parliament and incorrectly referred to her as a journalist (thereby risking her safety in Iran), Richard had to halt any plans he had on the campaign and take a step back. The storm that erupted as a result meant that there would be no use in doing or saying anything about the campaign until things were resolved. Instead, he spoke to the media about the importance of people knowing the truth, that Boris Johnson's comments were incorrect. He needed that to be heard in Iran, by the authorities, whom he knew were always watching what was happening in the UK. Ultimately, this helped the campaign because it led to Boris Johnson agreeing to meet with Richard. There was no way of knowing this was how it would pan out; if you really want to win, you have to be flexible to the environment and respond to it.

Sustain your supporters

Whether you're going through a quiet time in the campaign, or everything is kicking off, don't forget about your supporters. They are the key to winning this and will help you through the times when it feels tough to win. Whether you reach them on social media or email, keep every person who has joined you along the way in the know so that they stay with you to the end.

Campaigns can be mapped out with milestones,

smaller moments you need to win that will get you closer to victory. The trick is to report back on these and really celebrate them. Don't just keep your head down and slog away until you reach absolute victory – take a moment when an influential person or group backs your campaign to really shout about it. If you manage to get a great piece of press for the campaign, tell your supporters and ask them to share it. Treat each moment of success as just that – a real success! Something to be cheered, because you're not just applauding yourself, you're applauding your supporters who, in every action they have taken, have helped get you to that point. It's important because it shows your supporters, who aren't in the thick of the campaign with you, that victory is possible. Every small step taken makes winning far more tangible. It motivates people to take more action for you. And it's what strong community-building is all about.

Self-Care for Activists

'Caring for myself is not self-indulgence, it is self-preservation, and that is an act of political warfare.'

— Audre Lorde

I have a confession to make. As I write this chapter, I am wrapped up in a duvet with a cup of mint tea trying to show myself love after weeks of relentless juggling. Sleepless nights, coming down with a cold and going through phases of anxiety attacks have also been involved.

Even if you're not yet campaigning, you are probably exhausted by the state of the world right now. We're stuck in twenty-four-hour breaking news cycles and social media gives us no breaks. Politics feels like it's pretty nasty these days, with views becoming more polarised and debates less understanding. Climate change is a looming threat to our existence and it's difficult to know what we can do to save the planet. It's important that campaigning doesn't diminish your energy and hope, but adds to it.

Activism can be hard and overwhelming, especially when it's not your main job – but it doesn't have to lead to where I am now, in a depleted state of exhaustion. Which is why this chapter is so important – because campaigning is important work that we all need to do. But there are safe and kind ways to go about it, and there are relentless and draining ways that will consume you, leaving you less able to make an impact. If you are flicking through the book and this chapter stood out to you, it might be a sign that you should read this first!

Campaigning is personal

If you are speaking out about something you care deeply about, it will feel personal to you. Whether you're campaigning for yourself, a loved one or a wider cause, the sheer fact that you care enough to spend your time working on it means you really must care about it. Here's the strange thing: when we care, when our heart is really in it, we are both more powerful and more vulnerable than ever. That seems like a contradiction; if we are powerful, how can we also be in a vulnerable position? Earlier in the book I talked about the power of personal storytelling. That your experience and story gives you power that no one can challenge. This is true. But it can also make you feel vulnerable to the world. Revealing parts of yourself can feel scary, making you hyper-aware, looking for approval and rejection. The rejection is maybe not even there, but you try to find it anyway. And campaigning is tied up with who we are because it inherently represents our values. So when you are challenged, as you will be in your campaign journey, it can feel difficult because it can feel like your values are being challenged. It's OK to feel like this, and don't let it put you off campaigning. Just make sure you are taking care of yourself while you do it.

Creating boundaries

Asma Elbadawi is a basketball player, spoken-word poet and activist. Her activism takes the form of poetry (she writes and performs about her identity as a female Muslim basketball player, about masculinity and body image) and it has also seeped into her sport. In 2017 she campaigned for the basketball association FIBA to remove a ban on hijabs and religious headwear, and won. Asma is also Sudanese and as her platform has grown bigger, the demands for her to speak out on various issues have grown. Protests in Sudan started in 2018 over cuts to bread and fuel subsidies and then morphed into anger at former president Omar al-Bashir's rule, leading to calls for him to stand down. 'I was in Sudan but couldn't talk about what was happening out there (politically) on social media. But people didn't understand the situation and why that would have been dangerous. I got so many messages asking why I wasn't posting. You can't expect anyone with a platform to speak – it's not always safe.'

It's OK to draw boundaries. In fact, it's important to know what you can and can't do. If something feels like it's not right, trust your instincts and say so. Take care of yourself first and foremost. Asma said to me, 'I enjoy activism when it's coming from me, not when it's *expected* of me.'

Know who to turn to

Not everyone in your world will be able to relate to or understand how to support you when things get over-whelming. Know who the people are that you can turn to, and make sure you ask for help. Asma said that she doesn't get easily agitated but when she does, her close-knit group of friends is what gets her through. And as her platform has grown, she has friends in a similar position whom she can speak to and who she knows will understand.

'I get frustrated if someone can't see something from my point of view. For example, women's rights; when people start asking, "What about men's rights?" I find that level frustrating, when I have to explain why something is universal.

'I try to keep a close-knit group of friends who understand me as a person, not the campaigner but the one that cares and is funny and is a human. They are also all on social media. The more I get known on social, the less I can connect to my old friends, so I need them. There's one friend who I see, and we just meet to do our weekly shopping together. It's so nice, we just go around the shops, getting our food, and it becomes a therapy session.'

Amani Al-Khatahtbeh, Muslim activist and founder of Muslim Girl, a well-known blog for Muslim women, told *Self* magazine:

'In 2014, my first year out of college, I was taking part in a protest in Washington, DC. A bunch of counter-protesters showed up and targeted me. The things they said were dehumanising, hurtful, and traumatic. None of the other activists identified what was going on and instead pushed me to work harder. I totally burned out and stopped social justice work for two months.

'When I met up for coffee with another activist and told her what had happened, she identified that I had been triggered and needed self-care. That moment really showed me the importance of surrounding yourself with a good support system and other women activists with whom you can share the struggle.'

Both Asma and Amani have found that leaning on other activists has been a powerful source of support. In your campaign you'll come across others doing similar work to you; build these relationships as you'll understand each other and what you're experiencing more than anyone else can.

Find a mentor

When you're leading something like a campaign, it can feel lonely. Even if you have a great community of supporters and loving friends and family, you are still the person having to make decisions and push the campaign forward. Part of the stress comes from doubting yourself, not knowing if you're making the right decisions or going in the right direction. Even if you're not conscious of this doubt, it may still be there under the surface. This low-level stress can build and in the worst cases, make you unwell. That's what happened to me, and the moment I realised that the source of it was the heavy burden I was carrying, I looked for a mentor.

A mentor is someone who can advise and guide you. They can provide you with support through their own experience and networks. They are there to challenge you in a supportive way in order for you to grow. And most importantly, they can act as your cheerleader, someone who has the expertise and authority to tell you when you're on the right path.

To find your mentor, think about the people out there who are either doing similar work to you, but have more experience, or just someone you respect and admire. And ask them! Be very specific and clear on what you want out of the relationship, for example that you would like to meet them once a month for an hour to run campaign ideas past them. The worst-case scenario is that they are too busy or feel unable to take on a mentee at this time, but at least you've made the connection and they may be able to offer help in other ways later down the line. It's a flattering request for any potential mentor to be asked to help someone because of their experience or authority, so don't be scared to approach them; remember that you're giving them a compliment!

And once you have your mentor, make sure you do the heavy lifting. The mentor is giving you their time and wisdom; you need to be proactive in setting dates and coming to meetings with questions and topics you want to discuss. You will get out of it as much as you put in.

Channel it into your work

I love to write, and when I feel angry, frustrated, or upset, writing is my lifeline. There's something about pouring it out, expressing myself and also knowing that I can do something useful with that emotion, that I find helpful. Christian anarchist Elbert Hubbard, in a 1915 obituary for actor Marshall Pinckney Wilder, wrote about Wilder's optimism:

> *He picked up the lemons that Fate had sent him and started a lemonade-stand.*

Hence the phrase was born, 'When life gives you lemons, make lemonade.' This is what I do with my frustration. It feels good to write; whether it's a short story or a political blog, it makes the emotion feel like it's worthwhile. Asma does the same: 'When I get angry, I start by ranting to people close to me who I know won't judge and will listen. Once that initial anger has dissolved I'll channel it into a spoken-word piece or an art-related piece, or a social media post. I don't want to come across the wrong way, to be misunderstood, so it's important I talk it through first. I also go play basketball on my own, with headphones, and shoot hoops. I write poetry. I've started saying that poetry isn't just work because it's a way of coping too.'

If you come up against something that makes you mad, write about it. Get someone to proof and edit to check you've communicated your points well (and to tone down the caps and expletives, depending on how mad you are feeling). And then send it to your supporters or pitch it to a news platform. Make something of it. Your emotions are what people connect to, so there's nothing wrong with feeling tired or mad or sad. And when you start sharing these feelings with your community, you will see the power of solidarity, of those who support you coming forward, to hold you up.

Take time out

There will be times when channelling your feelings, or creating boundaries, won't work. And you just need to take time off (which is in its own way creating your boundaries). It's OK to take time off; in fact, you must, for the sake of your health and the future of your campaign.

Asma: 'I give myself time off from social media and emails for a few days. And I started saying no. People often want to collaborate with me and I've had to start saying no to those things. And unpaid events – I say no. I used to feel bad but I've realised I need to be mindful of my health first and then take other stuff on. It took me until the end of the FIBA campaign to realise I was tired – I was ten years of tired! My whole entire life had become about that campaign – I would wake up, there'd be emails, go to basketball and post about the campaign. My entire life became about it.'

It's so easy when you're doing something you're passionate about for it to seep into every crack of your life until you have no room left for yourself. But you are a precious resource that has to be protected. And nobody will do that; people who are asking things of you don't know what else you have on your plate. The responsibility to take time for yourself rests with you. If you feel overworked, and that your mental health is starting to be affected, learn to read the signs and take some time out. Some activists I know take a break from it all for a long period; the campaign, social media, reading the news, everything. They take time to connect with friends and do things in the real world like go for walks, sleep, read. Other people take breaks at specific times, like the weekend, or on Sundays. However you manage it, remember to do it. None of us is superhuman, we are all human beings that need to rest.

Dealing with social media and trolls

Social media is like a sibling you both love and hate. It can lift you up and make you feel like a hero. Social media has given us incredible access to influential people like journalists and decision-makers as well as being one of the best ways to mobilise support for your cause. But like any great sibling, it knows exactly how to make you feel like crap. It knows your weaknesses and how to exploit them. It is full of trolls (people who use the internet to post provocative messages to create arguments), it never stops, and it speaks to the human need for approval and to be liked – and it's never enough. It can increase anxiety, cause depression and make us feel like we're not good enough. So what do you do, when there's this tool that you need to help your campaign, but which can be damaging to your mental health?

Similar to the approach of taking time out, the way you engage with social media needs to have your self-care in mind. Asma is prolific on social media, she uses it as a channel to express her views and broadcast her art and activism. She predominantly uses Instagram to do this and has over 8,000 followers there. How does she manage it?

'One of the biggest learnings I had was don't look at the comments section! Whatever is written there is about your race, religion and what you look like. It's not about your views, people are looking to say things that will hurt your feelings.'

Trolls, or cyberbullies, are a strange phenomenon. They have grown in their numbers with the rise of the internet. The internet is an incredibly powerful force for good, and can help you, if you feel less confident in the real world, to have your say. But since people are less inhibited online and there is more physical and emotional distance between what you are saying and the recipient, this is also a recipe for destructive behaviour.

'People in public life have always faced abuse. The more traditionalist approach was for the tormentor to scribble together their rantings (preferably in green ink) and pop it in the post. It's quite a lot of effort, though: you need to buy envelopes and stamps, and then stomp off cheerfully to the nearest post box. Then email came along, making howls of abuse cheaper and speedier – though keeping your identity hidden is a bit fiddly. Today, thanks to social media, quickly and anonymously sending abuse has never been easier. If you have set up a Twitter account, you can tell someone to fuck off and die in seconds. And this is exactly what hordes of furious, frustrated individuals have done – scores of Twitter accounts have been created to hound, intimidate and abuse. Once, Angry Frustrated Man would screech and yelp at their television when their hate figure appeared. Now, they can beam their frothing hatred into the lives of their targets in an instant. These are popularly known in the cyberworld as "trolls".'

Owen Jones, for the *Independent*

Trolls generally want the attention, they get a buzz out of creating drama in open spaces and to be honest, I don't know if they always believe what they're saying. They're lashing out, trying to be seen and heard. It's often less about you, and more about their own insecurities.

But that doesn't make them any less harmful and distressing. Some people say, 'Don't feed the trolls.' That is personally my approach; I have had people tweet racist things at me when I have campaigned or spoken out about political issues. And I've had horribly sexist and bullying remarks directed at me in the comments section in blogs I've written. I have a general rule of not responding because I know myself and know that if I go down that rabbit hole, my energy will deplete and I will waste time on the wrong people. I also don't want to give that troll any more airtime or space by engaging with them.

Some amazing activists I know call out bad behaviour in brilliantly witty ways and basically out-troll the troll. You can do this by retweeting them, replying back and poking holes in their often flawed thinking. Taking a light-hearted approach in response can also act as a bit of self-care, in creating distance between you and the troll by not taking them seriously.

This is harder than it sounds though and I've certainly never done it. You should only engage in this way if you feel you can do so in a self-protective way.

Whether you engage or not, make sure you block them and report them. Every platform should have a 'report abuse' function. But if it's hate speech or threatens your safety, you should go to the authorities. People engaging in internet trolling are immediately committing an offence under the Malicious Communications Act 1988 and the National Police Chiefs Council have a new unit called the Online Hate Crime Hub, which focuses on internet trolls and online abuse. Once you have reported the troll to the platform, take a screen grab and any other evidence and contact your local police.

And don't listen to a word they say; remember, you are a brilliant person doing something wonderful with your life.

Some final thoughts on self-care for activists

Self-care isn't just about taking a bath or eating your fave food. It's realising that we're living in a time of overload, with more opportunities, access to information and demands on our time than ever before. It's putting your health – both physical and mental – before anything else.

Self-care for activists is:

- Turning your phone on airplane mode hours before you go to bed and reading a book.
- Declining that invitation to an important event because you've spent no time with your friends or family that week.
- Saying 'no' even if you think it will make someone upset with you.
- Listening to your instincts and then responding to them.
- Letting other people take care of themselves (rather than you trying to fix everything).

I asked Asma and Richard for some final advice on looking after yourself.

Richard: 'There are times when there is too much going on and I need to calm down, particularly with big decisions. So I stop, I slow down and go quiet and don't worry about the deadlines; that's my safety valve. For emotional support I'll see old friends and family, people who knew me and Nazanin before all of this happened. I can't keep a journal because it would open up a Pandora's box, but writing updates to the petition and telling our story has been therapeutic. There are also support structures out there, there's a hostage support charity where I have a caseworker. It's someone I go for a beer with who's been there and knows exactly what I'm going through.'

Asma: 'Face the world as though there are no barriers. It's interesting because I don't see my hijab, so I didn't see it as a barrier. If you think about the things that are supposedly holding you back, it can stop you from being your best self. I like the phrase, "Fake it till you make it." We know the barriers are there but act like they're not.'

So, You're an Activist Now . . . ?

Activist /ˈaktɪvɪst/ n: advocating or engaged in activism; someone who takes part in activities that are intended to achieve political or social change.

You care passionately about an issue and you're going to do something about it – that makes you an activist. Don't be scared to own that word, embrace it and be proud of it. You're taking a stand in a world where it is easy not to. Just because you're not getting arrested and scaling buildings, doesn't make you any less of an activist.

As you know by now, activism, or campaigning, takes many forms and they are all as legitimate as each other. I was at a party recently with some friends. The subject got onto the leadership of the Labour Party and whether or not Jeremy Corbyn was doing a good job. Almost immediately several friends quietened down, and took a back seat in the conversation. When I asked one of them about it afterwards, a friend whose views and opinions I admire and whom I learn from every time we speak, she said that it's hard to engage in 'political' conversations because there is a constant fear you don't know enough.

I empathised and could quite clearly see my younger self in that moment. When I was growing up in the Midlands, I remember being shut out of conversations by kids in the classroom, the bullies, who didn't want a girl, an Indian girl, to be heard. They were afraid of losing their power. The attention they commanded was a precious thing and they were reluctant to give it up. I see a similar dynamic play out when people are given the message that you have to be a certain type of person to talk about politics.

The truth is that it's not rocket science and everyone has a valid opinion, quite frankly because we are all affected by the work of politicians in our everyday life. As John Bercow said, politics is every inch of our lives. Politics belongs to all of us. And shutting out certain voices only serves those who are afraid of losing power.

Pass it on

Now that you know the basics, hopefully you realise it's not as hard as you might have thought. So pass on that wisdom, and all the things you know. We'll only build empowered societies that can create change when every one of us knows how to channel our own voice and build it into a collective strength. The next time someone is complaining about something in the news, ask them if they want to do something about it, and tell them how. And help those around you get involved in the campaigns in your community and on social media. Now you know how important every single supporter is to a campaign, and how hard it can be to lead the campaign without the help of the community around you, use your voice to help support others. If there is one thing I hope you take away from this book, it's that you are powerful and you are political, and you can *do something* if you really want to.

Campaign Checklist

Still unsure whether to begin a campaign?
Use this flowchart to get you started.

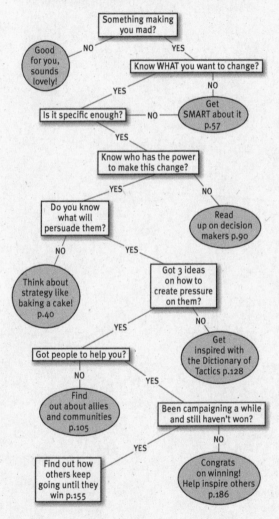

Acknowledgments

This book would not exist if it weren't for the activists who paved the way and inspired me to believe in the power of speaking up. People like Jayaben Desai, who deserve much more recognition. Nor would it exist if it weren't for the activists I know today, especially the Bears: Guppi, Hanna and Kash. You three have been so important for me and my understanding of justice. To my Change.org family, I adore you and learn so much from you all every day. To Ben especially. For creating a platform that has given voice to so many individuals who would not have been heard otherwise, a platform that has literally saved lives.

Jane Graham-Maw and Briony Gowlett – this book would not exist without you both believing in me and in the idea. Thank you for matching my passion and making the whole process as easy as possible for a fish out of water like me! And to the rest of the team at Hodder & Stoughton who have made this such a fun ride, Steven, Caitriona and Cameron.

KAJAL ODEDRA

Thank you Brie, for the foundations you built at Change.org UK, without which many of the stories in this book would not have been told. And a huge thank you to the people whose stories I have been lucky enough to be a part of, to help in some way and inspired to tell in this book; Laura Coryton, Yvonne McHugh, Ailbhe Smyth, Harriet Wells, Lindsay Garrat, Stevie Wise, Lucy Ann-Holmes, Caroline Criado-Perez, Yas Necati, Luke Wilcox, Belinda Bradley, Richard Ratcliffe, Magid Magid, John Bercow, Lucy Gavaghan, Kevin Smith and Asma Elbadawi.

Duncan, you helped in so many ways, but mostly I want to say thank you for having so much faith in me. I'm so glad you're a part of this. Penny for the words and Rosie for managing to squeeze a headshot out of me. Thank you to my family, Mum, Dad, Sheelah, Kam and Meenal. I love you all so much – thank you for putting up with the activist in the family. I wouldn't be the persistent little person I am now if it wasn't for all of you.

Index